HIDDEN TREASURES

EAST SUSSEX VOL II

Edited by Simon Harwin

First published in Great Britain in 2002 by
YOUNG WRITERS
Remus House,
Coltsfoot Drive,
Peterborough, PE2 9JX
Telephone (01733) 890066

HB ISBN 0 75433 964 5
SB ISBN 0 75433 965 3

FOREWORD

This year, the Young Writers' Hidden Treasures competition proudly presents a showcase of the best poetic talent from over 72,000 up-and-coming writers nationwide.

Young Writers was established in 1991 and we are still successful, even in today's technologically-led world, in promoting and encouraging the reading and writing of poetry.

The thought, effort, imagination and hard work put into each poem impressed us all, and once again, the task of selecting poems was a difficult one, but nevertheless, an enjoyable experience.

We hope you are as pleased as we are with the final selection and that you and your family continue to be entertained with *Hidden Treasures East Sussex Vol II* for many years to come.

CONTENTS

Dejuan Broughton	74
Grace Jenkins	75
Tom Cooper	76
Alice Johnson	76
Hannah Wain	77
Kyle Prangnell	77
Francesca Forde	78
Ashlyn Cahill	78
Alice Fuller	79
Emma Simpson	80
Alice Veal	80
Lana Castle	81
Emma Levett	82
Rianna Clark	82
Jessica Perry	83

St Mary's RC Primary School, Crowborough

Jessie Willis	83
Tyler Benton	84
Rosie Jones	84
Connor Scarlett	85
Thomas Mitchell	85
Shanagh Smith	86
Brian O'Connor	86
Charlie Nicoll	86
Natasha Beard	87
Tyler Andrews	88
Jojo Kyne	88
Harry Wrigley	89
Jonathan Townhill	89
Sam Morgan	90
Lydia Shepherd	90
Charlotte Edwards	90
Lydia Bannister	91

St Peter & St Paul Primary School, Bexhill-on-Sea

Lauren Smith	91
Jessica Elliott	92

Kieron Akam	92
Megan Milarski	93
Chloé Lusted	93
Aaron Pape	94
Jennie Warnett	94
James Taylor	95
Faith Young	95
Helen Johnson	95

Somerhill Junior School

Dominic Pearson	96
Dara Brown	97
Lucy Udeen	98
Rosemary Coogan	98

Stonegate CE Primary School

Ned Butcher	99
Lucy Jordan	100
Amy Smith	100
Jessica Steven	101
Tom Wortley	101
Henry Bramall	102
Toby Longhurst	102
Joseph Pocock	103
Megan Brickell	103
Fred Maynard	104
Sophie Mallion	104
Peter Snow	105
Millie Shreeve	105
Charlotte Wates	106
Alix Longhurst	106
Grace Lane	106
Mana Pettyl	107
Christophr Steven	107
Sophie Rolleston-Smith	107

Temple Grove School

Theo Briffa	108
Jack Vickers	108
Henry Mawhood	109
Larah Ann Charlesworth	109
Jessica Barrett	110
Ben Mundy	110
Sam Balcombe	111
William McCrow	111
Amber Jenkins	112
Charlie Dagwell	112
Jesse Asherson-Webb	113

West Hove Junior School

Danny Taylor	113
Jack Smith	114
Chelsea Richards	114
Louis Dodd	115
Jamie Milton	115
Georgina Cluett	116
Emma Peat	116
Blue Dean Keeter	117
Levi Ryder Bianco	118
Hannah Rhodes	118
Gavin Barsby	119
Yasmine Sebbah	120
Charlotte Janay Burton	120
Mason Horgan	121
Nadia Wareham	121
Harriet Massing	122
Daisy Penfold	122
Shanita Limbachia	123
James Murdoch	124
Aeron Corrigan	124
Lucy Donaldson	125

The Poems

FLYING

Her golden hair rushes past her warm, pale face
and her skirt flutters in the breeze.
She can see a rainbow in front of her
and a cat perched on a wall grooming itself.
She can't see the small ants and the puddles of mud
from the unforgettable rain soaking everything.
She can hear the singing of the birds in a tall tree
and a boy crying after falling off his bike.
She can't hear the weeping of an ant
that was nearly squashed to death by a naughty boy.
She can feel the cool breeze brushing against her face
as she glides through the air.
She can't feel the warm grass against her soft, pale feet
as she swoops to the ground to find she's sleeping.

Heidi Ottley (10)
Buxted CE Primary School

I WOULD LIKE TO . . .

I would like to paint an insect and the stars singing in the air.
I would like to touch a big rock, penguins' soft hair.
I would like to touch a big dragon's back.
I would like to touch a roaring lion.
I would like to hear the dark, misty, greyish fog.
I would like to hear the iron wolf rushing like the wind.
I would like to hear the rushing water going down the stream.
I would like to hear a ghost doing its ghostly sounds.
I would like to paint the frosty wind flying through the sky.
I would like to hear the thunder raging through the sky.
I would like to paint the raging sea crashing against the stones.

Ben Hall (10)
Buxted CE Primary School

SPACE BOMB

I am magnificent Mars
I am the hottest planet
I am making heat
I am to be red and dusty

I am magnificent Mars
I am to make some dust
I am all red and dusty
I am hot, you cannot stand on me

I am a glowing moon
A rocket zooms fast
I can see hot dusty Mars

I am a glowing moon
High in the sky
When I die . . .
The sun takes my place.

Georgina Barnard (10)
Buxted CE Primary School

LONG WALK

I have long walks in worlds unknown to you,
Jumping dolphins swimming in deep, black seas.
I go through a hole behind a bookcase,
Which leads me to an unknown world.

My best friends and I play together,
Playing is what we all do in our unknown world.

Laura Little (10)
Buxted CE Primary School

I WISH I COULD PAINT

I wish I could paint the noise of
a bee stabbing its victim.

I wish I could paint the noise of
a firing gun soaring through the sky.

I wish I could paint the noise of
a thunderbolt striking at a tree.

I wish I could see the thorn
stabbing a rose.

I wish I could see the wild horses.

I wish I could see the gold and silver wings
of an eagle.

I wish I had the most famous dress.

Lauren Newell (10)
Buxted CE Primary School

I WOULD LIKE . . .

I would like to see the peaky sound of the ant.
I would like to touch the shiny stars on the black blanket in the sky.
I would like to hear the sound of the sparkling sun behind the moon.
I would like to smell the beauty of the bark of a tree.
I would like to paint a picture of a face that lies in the sun.
I would like to paint the wind whistling through the leaves
                                        of the willow.
I would like to hear the song of the woodpecker's beak.
I would like to see the pandas eat bamboo without being hunted.

Tegwen Wilcox (10)
Buxted CE Primary School

Six Ways Of Looking At The Wind

The gentle and then hard wind
is a snake creeping to its prey and then striking.

The gentle wind is a butterfly
flying through the air.

A twister is a dinosaur
fighting another dinosaur.

The strong wind is an elephant
crushing everything that gets in its way.

The whistling wind is a cat
screaming as it echoes through the air.

An angry wind is a kangaroo.

Jamie Smith (10)
Buxted CE Primary School

Couch Potatoes

Couch potatoes, all they do
Is lay and whine
And stare at you
All they do is watch the telly
Sit and groan
Or fill their belly
That's all they seem to do
Nothing different
Nothing new
How boring their life must be
I'm so glad
That *I am me!*

Tanya Scanlon (10)
Buxted CE Primary School

SIX WAYS OF LOOKING AT THE WIND

The wild hurricane is a charging bull
wrecking everything in its path.

The confused typhoon is a gorilla
rampaging through trees, knocking them down.

The torrential monsoon is a snake
making tunnels through the leaves.

The gigantic tempest is a cheetah
speeding past bushes after its prey.

The wrecking cyclone is a mythical lion
moaning loudly in its sleep.

The speeding tornado is an elephant
storming through the forest.

Karl Thompson (11)
Buxted CE Primary School

SIX WAYS OF LOOKING AT THE WIND

The fierce wind is a ferocious lion,
The rage of the wind is a cheetah growling at its prey.
The swirl and whirl of the wind is like a worm
Weaving its way through the mud.
The howls and moans of the swirling wind
Are a hyena laughing.
The anger of the wind is the bull charging
And raging at you.
The blast of the wind is the trumpeting groan
Of the elephant.

Verity Daw (11)
Buxted CE Primary School

EVERY OTHER LETTER

A is for anagram,
     something quite hard.
C stands for cold,
     like Christmas cards.
E means everything,
     made in creation.
G is for goal,
     scored with celebration.
I stands for ink,
     all over my hands.
K means kite,
     swooping like doves.
M is for Mum,
     who I really love.
O stands for octopus,
     tentacles and legs.
Q means quiet,
     whilst I am in bed.
S is for something,
     that I don't know.
U stands for upwards,
     go, go, go!
W means wet,
     from the rain outside.
Y is for yacht,
     sailing by the tide.

Harriet Crawford (10)
Buxted CE Primary School

THE TOUCH OF MIDAS

One day in a land of old,
there was a king who could turn things gold,
he had the touch of Midas of course,
and turning things gold was his course.
He turned everything gold for hours,
plants, birds, even flowers.
Until he found he could not eat,
one little candy treat,
he found that everything turned to gold,
food, drink, even mould.
He turned his daughter into gold,
no one was safe in his strangle hold.
Wizards and wise men tried to get rid,
of the touch of Midas, they thought was putrid.
All of them failed, so the king went to the best,
the one who put the spell on him,
the one to beat the rest.
He found the wizard, oh yes he did
and he asked him nicely if he could be rid
of the spell he so much despised,
just for his family to be alive.
So he granted the wish that the king had made,
to rid himself of his terrible plague.
The spell was over,
his family alive,
plants, trees, flowers thrived.
So if you're ever offered the Midas touch,
just say no,
it will be too much.

James Jay Gordon (9)
Buxted CE Primary School

THE RACE

Waiting on the grid,
Tense petrol air,
Hands tightly on the wheel,
Eyes starting to stare.

Red, yellow, green,
The lights say go!
Jostle for places,
Must not be slow.

Foot to the floor,
Bend right, bend left,
Engine purring,
The crowd screams for more.

Overtake him, move near,
Moving up the pack,
Now in second,
Keep driving, watch for attack.

Round the last bend,
Look for the flag,
Just find more speed,
Yes, I passed him,

I've won!

Craig Crowther (9)
Buxted CE Primary School

WAR

My mind is empty, my aim is sharp
My knife is bloody and my throat is parched

My mind is empty, my sword is ready
My speed is fast and my sight is steady

My fist is strong, my suit is gold
My knees are weak and my heart is cold

My head is bold, my shirt is wet
My knife is bloody and my gun is set.

Tom Barnden (9)
Buxted CE Primary School

ONE DAY I FOUND SOME TREASURE

One day I found some treasure
I saw a sparkle
It caught my eye
I tried to get the treasure
It was stuck
It was wedged in a corner of a rock
So I went home to get a pickaxe
When I got back
It was gone.

Jamie Curd (9)
Buxted CE Primary School

MY HAMSTER

My hamster Harry, he is cool
and he sleeps all day.
He is great and full of fun.

My hamster Harry, loves his cage,
he spins his wheel fast.
He's round and fat, my best pal.

Kit Todd (9)
Buxted CE Primary School

THE GREAT JOURNEY

Three wise men on a great journey,
Following the star illuminated so clearly,
Riding camels to see a great child,
Now they are relieved that they are halfway there,
Bringing great gifts for the great child,
When they reach the small, dark stable
They are all excited that they have seen the newborn child,
They give the gifts of
Shiny gold,
Spicy myrrh
And powerful frankincense,
They pray to God in gratitude for what they have seen,
The new child,
The new king,
They bow, 'Oh Lord Emmanuel.'

Tim Newbury (10)
Buxted CE Primary School

ME AND THE MOON

Lying in my bed at night,
Startled by the moon so bright,
I climbed upon my knees to see,
Him smiling lovingly down on me,
Filling me with a warming embrace,
I stared back at him with a smiley face,
He took all my nightmares away
And he promised to visit another day.

Ellen Smith (9)
Buxted CE Primary School

Colours Remind Me Of . . .

Blue reminds me of the sea
Amber reminds me of a key
Orange reminds me of our cat
Yellow reminds me of my hat
Silver reminds me of a kite
Black reminds me of the night
White reminds me of my grandma
Gold reminds me of a star
Brown reminds me of our house
Grey reminds me of a mouse
Peach reminds me of my tummy
Pink reminds me of my mummy
Green reminds me of a tree
Purple reminds me of my friends and family
Turquoise reminds me of *me!*

Alice Todd (9)
Buxted CE Primary School

Flying

Majestically soaring, silently gliding,
I can barely see it at all;
The singing birds, the hunting cats,
But the ultramarine sky is astounding,
As are the fluffy white clouds
And the shining bright sun.

I imagine being down there,
Seeing rabbits bound through a field,
Climbing trees I can no longer see;
Then I coldly realise a longing, a hope;
To be on the ground enjoying again.

Joshua McLoughlin (10)
Buxted CE Primary School

FLYING

I can see empty fields,
towns with silent streets,
wild animals and the tops of buildings.

I can't see the birds on bare trees,
the people running on streets or cars speeding round corners.

I can her the birds whistle their morning song,
the sound of traffic and people muttering.

I can't hear the insects crawling around,
the sound of eggs hatching and animals charging around in circles.

I can feel the airy breeze of wind brushing against my face
and touch the fluffy clouds.

I can't feel an cold, icy lake and myself.

Adam Harris (10)
Buxted CE Primary School

ROBOT INVASION

Yesterday my house was invaded by robots,
They wrecked our house and our flowerpots,
They tied us up and watched TV,
We were scared, my brother and me.

Yesterday our house was invaded by aliens,
They were pink, red, blue and yellow,
I even saw a multicoloured alien,
They found some money and ran away,
I had to clear up all day.

Yesterday our house was invaded by Martians,
They found some food and sat down to eat,
We just knew we were dead meat.
They ran around and played games,
Then they started calling us names.

Tomas Messmer (9)
Buxted CE Primary School

IN THE PLAYGROUND

Running onto the playground
Everyone playing
Girls skipping
Boys playing football
Teacher drinking her coffee
Little girl lost and upset

Now the bell has gone
Silence, stillness
The second bell rings
Everyone walks to the lines
Teachers come to collect their classes
Now the playground is empty.

Elizabeth Wells (9)
Buxted CE Primary School

DRAGON CINQUAIN

Dragon
So cold but hot
All of fire but icy
Blazing eyes, abnormal, frozen
With fear.

Ellen Wise (10)
Buxted CE Primary School

I HAVE LONG WALKED IN WORLDS UNKNOWN TO YOU

I have long walked in worlds unknown to you,
Jumping dolphins swimming in deep black seas.
I go through a hole behind a bookcase.
My best friends and I play together
In a new land at last.
I am free from the throbbing noise of towns and cities.

Lynne Robinson (10)
Buxted CE Primary School

SIX WAYS OF LOOKING AT THE WIND

The angry wind is a troll, ripping up everything that gets in its way.
The dazzling fire wind is a dragon, shooting through the sky.
The fierce wind is a tiger tearing through the grass.
The angry wind is a golden sword cutting through the trees.
The dazzling wind is a spark of lighting zigzagging across the sky.
The angry wind is a whale tumbling through the sea.

Alex Tunna (10)
Buxted CE Primary School

SUPER GIRL

Super girl whizzing through the air,
She can sense danger miles away.
She can hear desperate screams for help,
She can see everything with her super dazzling eyes,
She can't hear the bubbles, the bubbles of a tiny goldfish
Swimming under the blazing sun.

She can feel the soft, fluffy cloud,
Shooting like a bullet past her delicate, peachy skin,
Her golden, brown, wavy hair blows everywhere.
Her rosy cheeks glimmer like cherries in the ocean sky,
But her beautiful face would scare the devil.

Oh how I wish I was her so badly!

Holly Hicks (11)
Buxted CE Primary School

I'D LIKE . . .

I'd like to see the tigers talking to themselves
In the hot, steaming depths of the jungle
And touch the pain of the Earth

I'd love to hear the history of time
I would like to smell
The blueness of the sky and ocean.

Oliver Conaboy (11)
Buxted CE Primary School

WAR

I think war tastes like hot curry
And smells like pepperoni pizza.
I think war looks like red blood,
I think hot war sounds like a volcano ready to burst
And lava comes out and spreads around Earth.

Daniel Robbins (9)
Buxted CE Primary School

THIS IS JUST TO SAY I'M SORRY

This is just to say
The other day
I ate your favourite curry
I am in a hurry
To buy you another curry
So I am very sorry
I ate your favourite curry
The vindaloo one!

I have brought you another curry
Still I am very sorry
It's in the fridge
Next to the figs
I need the loo
Now *sorry!*

John Wilson (9)
Buxted CE Primary School

SIX WAYS OF LOOKING AT THE TWISTER

The stormy twister is a rampaging rhinoceros
The violent twister is an eagle soaring silently around the atmosphere
The hissing twister is a snake sucking the defenceless rat
The cunning twister is a sleek cat spinning on its tail
The roaring twister is a powerful lion hunting the
                              blood-stricken wildebeest
The galloping twister is a mythical unicorn.

Max Lamb (10)
Buxted CE Primary School

CHAMELEON

Quick!
Move!
Stop!
A greenfly.
Tongue moves fast as an arrow.
Silently moving,
A swarm of flies.
Get to work.
Must move.
Fast!
Gone!
Catch!
Dead . . .
Caught and trapped
In a dark, wet, mouldy hole.

Eden Richards (9)
Charters Ancaster College

GOLD

A glinting shield
Shimmering in the moonlight.
Coins clattering.
Beetles with a deadly shine.
A sunflower in the light
Inside dark houses.
A bolt of lightning
Coming down to Earth.
A gold pen accidentally scratched,
Mixed with a patch of grey.

Matthew Pope (8)
Charters Ancaster College

THE MAGIC BOX

I will put in the box

Mischievous monkeys full of banana milkshake,
Shimmering ships sailing slowly across the sky
And shining sand horses as solid as stone.

I will put in the box

The sprinkled grass, green with dew,
Icicles hanging from the floor,
Freezing red and bubbling blue.

I will put in the box

Turquoise sand, dusted with the golden sea,
The silver sun and the golden moon
And the soft Milky Way like a bowl of whipped cream.

I will put in the box

Foghorns creeping across a misty sea,
Galloping white horses crashing into a cliff
And every single scent of the world.

The lid of my box is made from

The shimmering northern lights,
A flame from the fiery sun
And the dust of the silver moon,
Dancing across the sky.

In the corners of my box are

The voices of the blue whales,
Seashells from the seven seas
And the exquisite sunrise on a frosty morning.

In my box I shall
Dance with the mammals across the land
And swim with the fish in the deepest sea.

Jessica Collishaw (11)
Charters Ancaster College

TWILIGHT

High up in the sky
The sun is fiery.
Waiting,
Waiting for the moon
To come and she to go.
But while she is waiting,
She looks down,
She sees horses eating long, green grass.
Children playing,
Running across the fields.
The moon taps her on the shoulder.
It is time to go to bed.
Now the moon is watching,
The horses flying away,
With the stars in their manes
And the children are going home.

Everything
Sleeps.

Mollie Alcott (10)
Charters Ancaster College

THE WIND

Whistling like a steam engine,
Moaning,
Groaning,
Howling pitifully.
Leaves blown roughly,
The colours of sunset.
Crackling Rice Krispies.
Branches breaking and crumbling,
Dropping to the ground
From the bare, solitary trees.
Wind stretching out with invisible hands,
Stinging faces.
A raven, feathers glistening,
As dark as the night,
Soars overhead.
While emerald shoots sparkling with sapphires
Watch, swaying as the nonchalant wind blows by.

Sawan Bharj (9)
Charters Ancaster College

O°C

Frost on the icy branches
like the pointed end of spears.
The swimming pool is frozen
like an icy mirror.
The icy daggers are filled
with icy mud.
Snowflakes like frozen leaves
dropping from freezing trees.
Frost slowly dripping
off the silent trees.

Benjamin Hammond (8)
Charters Ancaster College

CHAMELEON

He's keeping on eye on you!

With a grin like a fox
And a mouth like a bear
He's planning a plot to get you!

He climbs back down
Onto the ground
And he's still got his eye on you!

He waits for his prey . . .
Look out, hey!
He's got you!

Then with a horrible smile
He climbs back up
To sleep for a while.

He's still keeping his eye on you!

Tristan D'Agar (8)
Charters Ancaster College

0°C

I see snowflakes fall
like lacy patterns so pure and white.
I see snow on the ground
like a soft, furry, frozen blanket.
I see frost on the treetops
like a pure white skeleton.
I see icicles hanging from big houses
like pointed spears.
I see lakes frozen
like shiny, sparkling mirrors.

Emma Bignell (8)
Charters Ancaster College

COLOURS

Red, the colour of the sun
When it is going down.
Warm, happy, cuddly.

White, the smell of popcorn.
The moon, shining.
A white panda.

Green, the wrapper of a sweet.
The scent of an apple.
The forest.

Orange, a light summer breeze.
A juicy orange.

Matthew Patterson (8)
Charters Ancaster College

SILVER

Silver is a strange sparkle in the moonlight,
A spreading beam of light,
A shivering thought,
A blinding light.
A piece of cuddly, warm cloth,
A dancing star
In the faraway distance.
An ice tree,
A frozen world.

Daniel Ogilvie (8)
Charters Ancaster College

CHAMELEON

Sly and cheeky,
Blue chameleon.
Slurping, pouncing,
Red chameleon.
Lazy, bumpy,
Pink chameleon.
Scaly, slurping,
Green chameleon.
Spiky, lazy,
Yellow chameleon.
Hungry and ready to
Pounce!

Henry Buller (8)
Charters Ancaster College

GOLD

Gold as the leaves in autumn
After a golden summer.
A beautiful, silky present
That you can't wait to open!
A golden pound, gold sweets.
Gold are the velvet flames
On a creamy cake.
It is warm.
The soft, pale, gentle light
On a summer evening,
Under the rainbow.

Rebecca Stewart-Hodgson (8)
Charters Ancaster College

THE MAGIC BOX

I will put in the box
Morning magic borrowed from the moon
Golden sunshine sparkling in the sky
And a wonderful world full of peace, not war

I will put in the box
Three golden promises that have to be kept
The last memory of the past pictured in my mind
And the future of tomorrow held in my hands

I will put in the box
An eternity of talking animals chattering cheekily
Three midnight dreams turned into the future
And five smiles illuminated by diamond mirrors

My box is styled with a child's emotions
And the lid is covered with voices of angels
The hinges are the worthy hopes of tomorrow
While in the corners are secrets never to be told

In my box
I will turn into the whirling wind
Which will take me to the heart of peace
Where the harmony will change the course
Of life forever.

Rosalyn Putland (10)
Charters Ancaster College

THE SCARAB OF POWER

The scarab of power is evil, not nice.
One day a madman tried to find the scarab, twice.
He failed first, but succeeded second.
This man had gusto, but no brains to match 'em.
The zombies woke up and attacked with power.
The madman fainted as quick as a dying flower.
He woke up in a tomb-sealed room.
He looked around, there was nothing there,
Except a statue saying 'Beware!'
He heard a sound, so he decided to get up and look around.
He found a switch, pulled it.
The room spun round just like a tube.
He found his way out. *Phew!*

James Hemsley (11)
Framfield CE Primary School

HIDDEN JEWELS

Hidden jewels you could find in the sea,
Hidden jewels, who knows where they could be.

Hidden jewels I could find today,
Hidden jewels, I don't think I can find them, no way.

Hidden jewels shining in the sunlight,
Hidden jewels glowing in the night.

Hidden jewels, I've found some I think,
Hidden jewels, green, yellow, orange and pink.

Hidden jewels I find in a chest,
Hidden jewels, they look the best!

Chloe West (10)
Framfield CE Primary School

TREASURE HUNT

Beep! Beep! Beep!
My metal detector went,
So over I bent,
There was something buried deep in the ground . . .

As I dug deeper,
My shovel went 'Clang!'
Then a noisier 'Bang!'
So loud, it would have woken a heavy sleeper.

My heart skipped a beat,
I jumped up and down,
Behaving like a clown,
My hands clawed at the peat . . .

What I saw,
Made me stare in awe,
I saw a chest,
Made of simply the best . . .
Wood.

I unlocked the latch,
With a flick of my hand,
Nobody had dug in *this* land!
Lighting a match,
I used the flame to peer inside . . .

I saw loads of gold!
Its colour was bold,
It looked very old
And felt icy cold.

I picked the chest up
And dragged it home,
It's still my secret . . .
Mine alone . . .

Matthew Molloy (10)
Framfield CE Primary School

THE MUMMY THAT WAS FORGOTTEN

The mummy that was forgotten,
dropped down to the bottom of the sea
and it was found by me.
Then I unravelled him and he said to me,
'Thank you for unravelling me,
I should be going now'
that's what he said to me.

We were flying over the sea,
like a bumblebee,
I spotted a shipwreck,
so I went under the sea.
I saw a treasure chest
and brought it to the surface
and broke the lock.
We shared out the money,
me and the mummy,
now we are
millionaires.

William Pegram (10)
Framfield CE Primary School

THE PLACE WITH A HIDDEN TREASURE

The air was cold and bitter,
there were bits of floating litter.

There were stars shining bright,
now the Earth was out of sight.

We reached a strange place,
never seen by the human race.

It looked a ghostly white,
the spaceship now seemed very light.

We hurtled through a rocky cloud,
a bang from the spaceship was very loud.

We landed by a huge rock,
that's when I saw a strange lock.

I stumbled over a lever,
then up rose a statue of a beaver.

There shone a dazzling beam,
it was the colour of bluey-green.

It held up a key,
that looked like the sea.

I placed the key into the lock,
which was near the huge rock.

There was a massive diamond,
so I took it back to our ship called Simon.

There was another bang which was loud
and I flew back through the rocky cloud.

I left the white ghostly place
and soared back into space.

I saw the stars that shone bright
and where the Earth is out of sight.

Back to where the air is cold and bitter
and where there's bits of floating litter.

Kellie Irwin (11)
Framfield CE Primary School

MY TREASURE

My treasure is big and small.
My treasure is happy and sad.
My treasure is good and bad.
My treasure is rich and poor.
My treasure is huge and strong.

My treasure can love and hate.
My treasure can open a gate.
My treasure can drink and eat.
My treasure can learn and grow.
My treasure can see and hear.

My treasure was born before time.
My treasure was great and bold.
My treasure was somehow created.
My treasure was a mystery or a secret.

My treasure will go on and on.
My treasure will be in the future.
My treasure will never die.
My treasure will live and live.

My treasure is life itself.

Tristram Macdonald (10)
Framfield CE Primary School

INTERESTING PLACES AND PASTS

In my loft is a treasure chest
In it was some dino bones
In it a pirate is a painting
From Henry II some gold and
From my cousin some silver from the seven seas
A club from a caveman
A glass from our Lord Jesus Christ
But there was nothing of me!
My gran was a Roman cooker
My grandad an artist
My aunt was a farmer
My uncle a builder on the island
My mother was a rider
My father a designer
My brother was our teacher
My great grandad's foot
For he was Long John Silver
But there was nothing in there about me.

Emma Cornwell (9)
Framfield CE Primary School

BURIED

There's buried treasure under the mud in my garden,
Under the bush which Mum put there,
I dug a bit yesterday, but the soil started to harden,
But I ran inside 'cause I saw a huge *bear*.

There's buried treasure under the mud in my garden,
I dug a bit more and I saw a *golden gun*,
It might have been Long John Silver's,
But who knows, I want to have fun.

Jack Conner (10)
Framfield CE Primary School

TEACHER VS ME

If I switched places with my teacher I would . . .
Sit in the staffroom,
While she puzzled over maths,
Drink my hot coffee,
While she struggled in SATs.
If I switched places with my teacher I would . . .
Sit comfy in a chair,
When she stood, cold,
Look after children,
When she tries to make poems bold.
If I switched places with my teacher I would . . .
Talk to other teachers,
While she was doing homework,
Know school surprises,
While she tries to lurk.

But then I'd tell her off,
For trying to skip school.
Now she'll be sad,
Instead of thinking it's cool!

Jessica Rose (10)
Ninfield CE Primary School

WHY IS IT ALWAYS ME?

Why is it always me who goes to bed first?
Why is it always me who never has chips and beans?
Why is it always me who gets to school last?
Why is it always me considered as a horrid friend?
Someone tell me, why is it always *me?*

Elsa Crouch (10)
Ninfield CE Primary School

HOMEWORK STINKS!

H orrible stuff homework,
O f course it's the worst thing in the world.
M um always tries to help me,
E xcept it gets me really twirled.
W hy do we have homework?
O h please, please tell me why?
R ough stuff, that's homework,
K or, I'd rather die.

S illy stuff is homework,
T he teacher thinks it's good!
I 'm suffering from homework,
N ever, ever like it so I'd burn it like wood.
K ill me if you please,
S till got homework disease.

I hate homework!

Alex Collishaw (9)
Ninfield CE Primary School

WHAT AM I?

I use my tail
To propel me through water,
My jaws are used for slaughter.
My diet is people and buffalo too
And sometimes my home can be in a zoo.
So you better think quick
Or you will be gone.
What am I?

A crocodile!

Steven Franks (10)
Ninfield CE Primary School

INFINITE MONEY

If I had infinity pounds
I would buy the school,
All the chocolate in the world,
A big huge pool
And a giant dartboard.

I would buy a brand new car,
A brand new house,
I would drink a beer in a nearby bar
And I would raise a mouse.

A brand new watch,
A TV with Sky,
I would get a fishing rod and a fish would I catch,
I would buy bug spray to kill that fly.

Christopher Bloomhill (10)
Ninfield CE Primary School

UNDER THE SEA

U nder the ocean
N ear the sharks
D eadly creatures
E ver dark
R ed-hot breath

T hey look so mad
H elp!
E lectric eels swimming

S eals by my face
E ating humans for their dinner
A ll around me sea creatures.

Alec Feakes (10)
Ninfield CE Primary School

THE WALKOVER

Wow, on a brilliant match like this
Arsenal are 3-0 up already
Although 5 exciting minutes have gone
Oh great, trust Arsenal to miss

Come on Arsenal, come on Arsenal
Wiltord, Henry and Bergkamp
All playing well . . . Pires on the ball
Yes . . . what a goal

Leeds are on the ball
Wright the keeper, should make a good save
Yes . . . he has saved the ball
Leeds are 4-0 down

The final whistle has gone
What a brilliant match
Henry 2, Wiltord 2 and Pires 1
What goals they scored.

Corey Scott (11)
Ninfield CE Primary School

IF ONLY

If only I didn't have to bother
With boring old school
I would go out to the sea
It's easy for me

I could breath underwater
I could have a room of chocolate
A servant as well
So it's easy for me

If only I could have
A portable dirt track
A portable farm with horses
That makes it easy for me

If only people would listen to me
And my ideas
Now they will
It's easy for me.

Alex Mitchell (10)
Ninfield CE Primary School

A WORLD MADE OF CHOCOLATE

Can you just imagine,
A world full of chocolate,
Caramel, toffee,
But definitely no nuts?

Just imagine if your house and school
Were made of chocolate,
Hot chocolate ran out of the taps,
The walls were made out of flapjacks.

In my chocolate world,
All the road
Is paved with Smarties.

I can't stop saying chocolate,
Someone help me please,
I think I've got chocolate disease.

April Fusco (9)
Ninfield CE Primary School

UNDER THE SEA

Under the sea
I can see the sand brush me,
I can feel slimy fish
Slipping through my hand.

Under the sea
I can see a fish eating,
I can see seaweed tangling
Round my feet
And the sea giving me a beating.

Under the sea
I can feel starfish sticking to me
And the dirt coming from the bottom of the sea.

Natalie Donno (11)
Ninfield CE Primary School

IN MY BED AT NIGHT

In my bed at night,
I can hear the whistling of the wind.

In my bed at night,
I can see the toothless grin of my wardrobe.

In my bed at night,
I can feel the spiders creeping up my neck.

In my bed at night,
I can taste the salty water of the sea outside.

In my bed at night,
I can smell the burning of the tyres from cars.

Hamish Hiscock (9)
Ninfield CE Primary School

MUSIC IS COOL

Music is cool
It has always ruled
I don't like pop
I like modern rock
I'm in a band
I'm the singer
I'm not like Babar Sprax
He's a minger
I like Slipknot
Limp Bizkit
And the legends, Queen
They're all good singers
They're all really keen
Music is cool
It has always ruled
I don't like pop
I like grunge rock.

Toby Strange (10)
Ninfield CE Primary School

CHRIS, THE MOOSE

I am a moose and Chris is my name,
I live in the wild but I'm really quite tame.

It gets very lonely out here on my own,
Dreaming of someone who might take me home.

Last week I got stung by a bee,
So can somebody please help me?

Michael Farrier-Twist (10)
Ninfield CE Primary School

UNDER THE WATER I FEEL . . .

Under the water I feel like a mermaid
Gliding through the sea,
But I'd better be careful
Because that shark's looking at me!

Under the water I feel like a dolphin
Leaping in the air,
Sliding along the surface
Without any cares.

Under the water I feel free,
Like I'm flying,
Swimming along happily,
On my back I am lying.

Oh well, it's only a dream
But it seems so real to me.

Rebecca Dalton (9)
Ninfield CE Primary School

IF I WAS . . .

If I was a billionaire, I would buy a silver metallic Mercedes-Benz.
If I was a billionaire, I would buy Chelsea Football Club.
If I was a billionaire, I would buy a mansion with twenty bedrooms.
If I was a billionaire, I would buy a million sweets.
If I was a billionaire, I would sail around the world five times.
If I was a billionaire, I would buy a ticket to the moon.
But Mum said I would have to put it in the bank!

James Broadbent (10)
Ninfield CE Primary School

BENEATH THE SEA

Beneath the sea
I can see
A rubbery back of a dolphin
Playing with me.

Under the sea
I can hear
A scaly fish
Bubbling in my ear.

Beneath the sea
I can feel
A silver tail
Of a seal.

Under the sea
I can smell
A shark with bad breath
Trying to eat a shell.

Beneath the sea
I can taste
Horrible sea water,
Rubbish and waste.

Sasha Austin (10)
Ninfield CE Primary School

THE LOFT

I got up one morning
And got out of bed,
I hugged my ted.

I didn't feel like work,
Instead I visited my mum,
I drove away.

I was there at my mum's,
I hugged her and she said,
'Can you clean out my loft?'

I went up to the loft,
I saw a huge box,
I looked inside.

There were lots of old toys,
I went downstairs to my mum,
She said that is a *treasure*
From my childhood.

Paul Cook (10)
Parkside CP School

MY COMET

Laying on the grass at night,
I look up at the cloudy sky.
Wishing to see a star so bright,
Knowing the comet will soon fly by.

The roof of the world was blank,
I'd searched it for many an hour.
After a while, all my hopes sank,
My expression soon became sour.

Searching the skies yet again,
The clouds had gone, the skies had cleared,
Across the sky as fast as a train,
My wish had then appeared.
I'd seen it at last,
Halley's Comet.

Hayley Froggatt (11)
Parkside CP School

MY SPECIAL MOMENT

One day when the sun had just set,
I dived under the glistening sea.
The sparkling fish swimming by,
Sharks hunting down their prey.
Minutes gone by, I spotted something,
Something unusual,
Something I hadn't seen before.
A shell of some sort,
Swimming deeper I reached out my hand,
Clutching it, I swam back up to the surface,
Taking my first breath.
Laying this cold, misty, shimmering shell on my boat,
I searched for a sharp rock.
Chiselling with flint it parted,
Anxiously I peered inside.
To my surprise it was not alone,
I couldn't believe my eyes.
There were several of them,
Looking at them hopelessly,
I realised it was cruel to keep them all.
I released all of the pearls,
But I kept just one,
To remember this wonderful time.

Samantha Bainbridge (10)
Parkside CP School

CHANGES IN NATURE

The egg is laid,
Though not hatched.
Caterpillar will soon pop out,
Munches the leaves,
Its belly fills up.
It might burst soon!
Changing to be a pupa,
Ties herself to a leaf,
Makes a cocoon around her.
Soon she will be beautiful.
The time is up,
She comes out of her cocoon,
A beautiful butterfly
And flies off into the distance.

Laura Woodgate (10)
Parkside CP School

SURPRISE, SURPRISE

Whilst on a sea
Faring quest

I found some coins
In a chest

The coins were
All soggy

Like a waterlogged
Moggy

They were chocolate
And that kind's the best!

Jack Cooper (10)
Parkside CP School

I Plant My Treasure Within The Seed

Out into the world it goes
The seed from inside the packet
I gently rake the soil on top
And wait for it to start growing
Today I look out upon my patch
To where my seed was planted
There I see a little green shoot
The growing process has started
I look out upon my plant
I see the flower head
It brings colours of red and blue
And I see its long green shoot
Today I can't see my plant
Where has my flower head gone?
I run out into the garden
And see it lying dead on the soil.

Hannah Sowten (11)
Parkside CP School

Back Safely

We were running through the field,
When the bright daffodils looked at me,
Then I looked into the sharp grass
And I saw something like brass.
I reached out my hand,
As if I was very grand,
I wondered what it was,
My eyes peered in, just like a pin.
Then I saw my old locket,
With my mum and dad inside,
Then I put it back safely in my pocket.

Jade Blackford (11)
Parkside CP School

SHOOTING TREASURES

I'm looking out of window, looking at the sky,
When all of a sudden I think I see a shooting star pass by.
It's all silver, it's all white,
It's travelling round the Earth tonight.
Showers of light push through the clouds,
All the sparks are tumbling down.
Just for one second, one blink of an eye,
I think I saw a miracle tonight.

It's all around me, rays of light,
Filling the darkness of the night.
A hidden treasure is coming out,
There's more of them than I can count.
After a while the showers die down,
They make a shape just like a frown.
Disappointment engulfed my mind
Of this hidden treasure I'd just started to find.

Yasmin Tivey (11)
Parkside CP School

OLD TED

When I went in Mum's attic,
I saw something quite ecstatic,
It was old ted that slept in my bed,
He went everywhere with me, he even went in the bath.

But then I grew up and ted went up,
Up to that gloomy old loft.
Put in a box,
Taped up,
Till I discovered him.

Adam Dudley (11)
Parkside CP School

SUMMER DAYS

Summer days, the spring gets left behind,
So we all can have fun in the new season.
We can all go to the fantastic beach
In the warm, beautiful sun.
Some will go on holiday, some will do many things
Before the season changes to autumn,
Where the wind blows the leaves along the round ground.
Summer days are a time to go in the scorching sun outside
And not inside because it is not that much fun.
Summer days are a time to go in the paddling pool
And have fun or pick flowers from the spring.
The seasons are spring, summer, autumn and winter,
But the season I like best is the summer days in summer.
Summer days are a time to have ice cubes in drinks.
Summer days are a time to have a water fight.
Summer days are a time to chill out in the garden.
Summer days are a time to have a scrumptious picnic.
Summer days will never be the same again.

James Clark (8)
Pebsham CP School

HIDDEN TREASURES

In the wild, overgrown jungle,
I wander slowly through the dangling vines.
As I look up I see that they look like Christmas decorations.
Pushing them from side to side,
As a beam of light came across my eyes,
I found a treasure box with jewels beside it.
I looked inside it,
I found a time capsule,
With the most shiny gold in it.

Brian Newman (10)
Pebsham CP School

HIDDEN TREASURES

In a wreck
On an island
Below the deck is a passage
Along that dark passage
Sticks out the head of a shark
There is slimy seaweed dangling from the ceiling
Down a trapdoor there sits a skeleton holding a sword
I can see something shining in his skull
I break apart his skull with the sword
There I find diamonds, jewels and gold
I'm rich, I say in my head
I put the glistening treasure in my pockets
And go out because it's starting to get cold
The lovely treasure is heavy and old.

Darren Clark (10)
Pebsham CP School

HIDDEN TREASURES

I stepped out into the fresh air of the morning.
Slowly I stepped over to the spade.
I picked up the spade and started to dig.
The digging went into a rhythm.
Suddenly there before my eyes was a rusted box,
Like a grey, dull postbox.
A door suddenly sprang open when my finger touched it.
Inside was a bundle of glistening coins,
Like a heap of Christmas chocolate money.
Was it real?
Yes! It was solid gold coins!

Jessica Mackenzie (9)
Pebsham CP School

HIDDEN TREASURES

The crumbs had mouldy marks,
Banana skin was all black and brown,
It looked like burnt sausages.

There were red stains on the floor,
Like ketchup.
Paper screwed up,
Like a screw in the wall.
There was one thing that looked good,
It was a sort of treasure.
It had coloured plastic stickers that looked real,
It was a necklace.

What is that shining underneath my smelly socks?
It shone like the sun on a warm, sunny day.
I threw away the smelly socks.
Then a blinding light shone.
It was a diamond, a green diamond!

Sherelyn Emery (10)
Pebsham CP School

HIDDEN TREASURES

T   he creepy cellar is dark and spooky.
R   ustling noises in the distance – is it bats?
E   erie feelings surround me
A   nd it felt very scary.
S   uddenly I see a light, it got bigger and bigger.
U   nable to move or see.
R   eaching out of the light, I fall down a deep, dark cave.
E   verything was glistening in the darkness.

Ian Mabb (9)
Pebsham CP School

HIDDEN TREASURES

In a cold, dusty attic where no one goes,
There are old, broken boxes piled up high.
As they touch the ceiling they looked like a mountain.
They were covered in thick layers of dust, just like white snow.
Then in the corner of my eye, a small box stood alone,
With cobwebs shining on the corners as frozen icicles.
Slowly I walked over to the box and wiped off the sticky dust.
I carefully picked up the broken box
And put it up to the ray of light.
The box was old and tatty,
With small holes and teeth marks showing.
I opened the tatty, old box.
The inside was covered in cobwebs.
Under the smooth cobwebs was an old picture,
Staring at me – but with no eyes.
The dust made me sneeze,
The dusty, old picture was the face of a human.
The face was very old.
I couldn't see who it was – the paint had melted away,
But it will be my treasure forever.

Lee-Anne Rodgers (10)
Pebsham CP School

THE MERMAID

I am a mermaid, I live in the sea,
But I am very beautiful,
But I'm kind, so pleased to meet you,
You must go now, so I can clean the sea
And when it is clean you can come
Under the glittery sea.

Hazel Holland (9)
Pebsham CP School

HIDDEN TREASURES

I walk out of the back door
When the sun shines.
I smell the summer breeze.
I walk further and further.
Then I see all the pretty flowers dancing
To the sound of the wind,
Swaying like the pendulum on a big grandfather clock.
I imagine sitting with my family in a field of love,
Skipping through the overgrown grass like a bird
Flying swiftly through,
Then going up into the tallest tree and feeding its young.
Not saving any food for itself, caring for its babies,
Like our mums do for us.
It doesn't matter if you don't get gold or pearls,
It matters that it came from the heart.
The best treasure you could have is your family.

Shiree Hillman (10)
Pebsham CP School

HIDDEN TREASURES

I went under, all I saw was a black mist.
When I reached the bottom, I saw yellow and blue plants.
I thought there would be nothing there.
Then suddenly I saw some brightly coloured fish with black spots.
I swam further through mists of black fish,
Past man-eating sharks with red blood on their lips.
Then I saw a boat, quite rusty.
I went inside and saw a bright yellow speedboat.
I took it and sped around the big blue waves.
I dived back and put it in a hiding place.
I come back every day now.

James Copeland (10)
Pebsham CP School

HIDDEN TREASURES

I knew it was somewhere
I'd searched everywhere
A red velvet box with beauty, dusty and old
I'm sure I put it in my drawer
But no, it wasn't there
Then I remembered the sofa . . . of course!
It was dark and scary
Then I felt something hairy
If it was there, it must be at the very back
Where thick dust layers the floor
I felt something there
I felt dizzy with joy
I felt the warmth at last
But it was just a sock
It gave me a shock!
I pushed it out of the way
I was fed up
Fed up with this hassle
My hair waving as I searched
Then I asked to pull the sofa forward so I could see
I saw it, excited!
I knew it was there
I took it out and blew the dust
It opened with a creak
Six generations had worn this in our family
Jewellery!

Zoe Willis (9)
Pebsham CP School

SPRING

Spring is a rich time,
Lambs play happily.
Birds sing sweetly
And calves are born quickly.

Children go out fishing,
Looking at the rain.
Parents do the washing up,
Wishing they could go out again.

Rosetta Mondel (8)
Pebsham CP School

THE DUKE'S BALLROOM

I was dancing in the Duke's ballroom,
When a ghost offered some perfume,
So I shouted out 'Shoo'
And painted him blue,
But he couldn't have been real, I presume.

Amber Hayler (9)
Pebsham CP School

HIDDEN TREASURES

In my bedroom there're probably twenty drawers,
I don't know where the present is.
Has my dog got it between her paws?
If my dog has it, it will probably be in the garden.
I need to get it now
Because it's my sister's birthday tomorrow.
I will have to give it to her next year.

That's if the dog doesn't get it first!

Coral Neale (10)
Pebsham CP School

MY LIFE

I was out at the shop
And then I heard someone crying,
What she said was sad,
Her uncle was dying.

So I comforted her,
Until she was alright
And when she stopped crying,
It was a nice sight.

That lovely girl,
She was me,
I got through to myself
And now my uncle's fine, see.

Kirsty Hoggins (8)
Pebsham CP School

MY DOG, JAKE

My dog, Jake is such a flake
You would really love him

Dalmatians are spotty,
Of course he's rather dotty,
Giving him cuddles all day.

Jumping up at cats
And taking him for walks.
Kicking balls he likes to do,
Even though he can't talk.

Ashleigh Rowe (9)
St Leonards CE Primary School, St Leonards-on-Sea

MY FAMILY

My family are nuts,
They're silly, they're nuts.

My family are crazy,
They're stupid, they're crazy.

But they're . . .

My family are kind,
They're gentle, they're kind.

My family are generous,
They're sweet, they're generous.

But I . . .

But I know,
They're the best thing that's ever happened to me!

Georgia Briggs (10)
St Leonards CE Primary School, St Leonards-on-Sea

MY DOG, SAPH

My dog, Saph is one of a kind
She just keeps appearing in my mind
She sleeps like a log
Even though she's a dog
But that's OK with me
And if I were to replace her
I would truly be insane
Because she's my dog, Saph
And I love her all the same.

Hannah Field (9)
St Leonards CE Primary School, St Leonards-on-Sea

CHOCOLATE

There's only one way to describe
chocolate and that is yummy,

As it trickles and slides
into my tummy.

It smells so sweet and looks so sickly,
probably because I ate it too quickly.

From strawberry to fudge
to coffee cream,

when I eat these
it makes me dream.

Of a trip to Cadbury's land.
When they give you chocolate
that melts in your hand.

Chocolate is given for many reasons,
especially at Easter and the festive seasons.

To end this poem there's
just one word to say,

chocolate is the best way
to end my day.

Chris Diamond (9)
St Leonards CE Primary School, St Leonards-on-Sea

MY ANNOYING BROTHER

I have an annoying brother,
He just loves his cover.
He called his father,
To take him to his mother's.

He eats like a pig,
He likes to dig.
My brother likes to play with kids,
His friend's name is called Sid.

Danielle Butters (9)
St Leonards CE Primary School, St Leonards-on-Sea

ALL ABOARD THE ANIMAL ARK

Tiger's fur blazing like flames,
Stripes like smudged ash,
Eyes like pearls,
Teeth like blades,
Its claws pack a powerful slash.

Elephant's trunk as long as a pipe,
Skin as grey as a rock,
Feet like pillars,
Nails like stones,
Stomping around the block.

Parrot's beak like shining gold,
Feathers as smooth as silk,
Wings like rainbows,
Tail like velvet,
Eyes as white as milk.

Fox's tail like a brush,
Nose as wet as a lake,
Paws like cushions,
Ears like spikes,
Fuss it cannot take.

Stacey Birch (10)
St Leonards CE Primary School, St Leonards-on-Sea

THE UNKNOWN POEM

I feel like writing a poem,
But I don't know what to write.
I asked my baby brother,
But he just started a fight!
When I turned to Dad and Mum,
Mum was always busy,
Dad was feeling glum
And so was my big sissy.
But now I'm stopping my poem,
For a very good reason indeed,
I've got no words on the paper.
I need help! Help! I'm in need!
Hang on a minute . . .
What's this on the paper?
While I've been telling you all of my caper,
I've written a poem,
A poem I've wrote,
No autographs please,
No need for a quote!

Stacey Amer (10)
St Leonards CE Primary School, St Leonards-on-Sea

JOE'S TOE

I have a friend called Joe
He always bites his toe
It got very sore
His mum shut it in the door
She said, 'I am sorry'
And she gave him a lolly.

Connor Mulvey (10)
St Leonards CE Primary School, St Leonards-on-Sea

MY RAP

I look cool in a back-to-front cap
My hands clap
My feet tap
I'm Jessica, I like rap
My best rap is my rap
I look cool in back-to-front cap
I like raps, it is cool, I like them
Because they are cool, I like caps
I like cool caps, they look cool on me
I really look cool in a cap cos they are wicked
My raps are cool and I look cool in a back-to-front cap
My favourite rap is my rap when I wear my cap
But I really wear my cap at all times
Caps are my best things to wear
They are cool, they are my best thing to buy
It is wicked, I like raps the best
Raps are my favourite thing
I can rap, I can rap, I can sing.

Jessica Morrissy (9)
St Leonards CE Primary School, St Leonards-on-Sea

A MAN FROM JAPAN

There was a man from Japan
Who wasn't really a man
He wanted to play football
But he wasn't really cool
That foolish man from Japan.

Anthony Clevett (10)
St Leonards CE Primary School, St Leonards-on-Sea

IN MY WORLD

In my world
I would like
Only girls (well a few boys of course)

In my world
I would like
A best friend

In my world
I would like
To eat chocolate for my tea

In my world
I would like
Sweets for my breakfast and for lunch

In my world
I would like
To be *free!*

Laura Jackson (10)
St Leonards CE Primary School, St Leonards-on-Sea

CHOCOLATE CAKE

Chocolate cake I adore
I want more and more and more

Chocolate cake with chocolate topping
Mum to bake and I will eat without stopping

Chocolate cake is so yummy
Bubbling in my big, fat tummy.

Catherine Turner (10)
St Leonards CE Primary School, St Leonards-on-Sea

ME

I am Lucy, I am really juicy
I am also really mmm, moosey
The boys seem to always be after me
I am obviously the one to be

I have a favourite song
It is called 'Where You Belong'
I like to boogie lots
And eat lemon sorbet out of pots

I'm tall and slim
I'm goin' out with a boy called Jim
He likes his food, he likes to eat
So at the restaurant we shall meet

I have long hair, it's nice and fair
All my friends are jealous, but I don't care
My brother always takes the mick
But I just sit there eating a lolly off a stick

After that my brother goes and plays the drums
And I just sit and chew the fingernail on my thumb
And then we both go to bed
Just like my mum had said.

Lucy Duffy (10)
St Leonards CE Primary School, St Leonards-on-Sea

THE BOY FROM SPAIN

There was a young boy from Spain
Who was completely insane
He met a girl and went in a whirl
That was the end of the boy from Spain.

Paul Reid (10)
St Leonards CE Primary School, St Leonards-on-Sea

MOUSE

Mouse going round
And round looking for
Some cheese.

Mouse going round
And round singing
High and low.

CH: Mouse going round
And round getting
Really tired now.
I want to go to bed
And spin around
Tomorrow.

Mouse going round
And round waking
Up so early.

Mouse going round
And round singing
Even higher.

CH: Mouse going round
And round getting
Really tired now.
I want to go to bed
And spin around
Tomorrow.

Rebecca Benge (10)
St Leonards CE Primary School, St Leonards-on-Sea

KISSING

Kissing in the corner
Kissing in the street
Kissing with the people that we meet

Big smoochie kisses
Pecks on the cheek
Sometimes people take a peek!
Aimee kisses James, it will come up in flames
Chloe kisses Oli underneath the holly
(Sorry no mistletoe)

Lucy kisses Jamie, although he fancies Amy
Amy hates him, she says he's too slim
Jamie is sick
Lucy runs quick
Miss comes in with a great grin
She says, 'What have you been doing?'
Darrell says, 'Yuck, this does suck!'

Liam kisses Megan
She thinks she's in Heaven
But we're all in Devon
Stacey kisses Ben, she's in love again

Kissing in the corner
Kissing in the street
Kissing with the people that we meet

Kissing!

Chloe Hinxman (9)
St Leonards CE Primary School, St Leonards-on-Sea

THE DOG RAP

He ran down the garden, he plodded down the street,
He wagged his tail, as he stamped his feet.

He jumped up the hill and chased a cat,
Where he saw a man wearing a green and blue hat.

Then he saw a bone and picked it up,
He plodded along and saw his friend, Pup.

When he went along with his friend, Pup
And they saw a little girl with a cup of soup.

So the little girl held out her hand,
They skipped along past a coconut stand.

Chloe Harmer (9)
St Leonards CE Primary School, St Leonards-on-Sea

WHAT IS PINK?

What is green?
An emerald is green in the starry stream.

What is yellow?
A lemon is yellow lying in a huge meadow.

What is red?
The sun is red in its universe bed.

What is gold?
Why gold is gold.
Yes gold,
Just gold.

Kristina Terry (9)
St Leonards CE Primary School, St Leonards-on-Sea

SCHOOL (A PRISON)

I enter school, I enter a prison
Where bad behaviour is forbidden
Where all slaves are under strict rules
All under the watchful eye
This is a place where sad faces pass by

The captains are called teachers
The leader is called a head teacher
To them we're all bugs and creatures
All they say is, 'Work faster, faster'

Phew! It's home time
I run for the gate
I have to get out
Can't be late
Phew, I'm through!

Alex Collins (9)
St Leonards CE Primary School, St Leonards-on-Sea

FIREWORKS

Fireworks go crash, smash, flash
In the black sky
Fireworks go sizzle, swizzle, drizzle
In the dark night
Fireworks go whizz, fizz, zizz
But I like fireworks when they go
Crash, smash, flash, sizzle, swizzle, drizzle
Whizz, fizz, zizz,
Bang!

Aimee Bourne (9)
St Leonards CE Primary School, St Leonards-on-Sea

BIRD

I am awake,
I get up,
I flap my wings,
I fly away,
I stop,
The wind carries me along the icy sky,
I am hungry,
I fly down to the normal world,
I find some people,
They feed me some chips,
I am thirsty,
I find a dog bowl with some water in it,
I drink it,
I fly away,
I am flapping . . .
Flapping my paper-like wings,
I fly home,
I see a human,
He is carrying a gun,
I figure that he is a *poacher!*
I fly as fast as I can,
I safely get home,
At last.

Ben Harrison (9)
St Leonards CE Primary School, St Leonards-on-Sea

BEST FRIENDS

Best friends comfort you
Best friends tell you secrets
Best friends are never horrible to you
Best friends play with you
Best friends play with you

Best friends are funny
Best friends have tickle tummies
Best friends help you with problems
Best friends are friends
Best friends are friends.

Megan Young (10)
St Leonards CE Primary School, St Leonards-on-Sea

MY WHITE RABBIT

My rabbit likes to eat food
And sometimes she is rude
Whenever she's around
All the cats want to pound
My rabbit is very white
And sometimes she can bite
So take my advice
She will eat mice.

Emily Rowland (9)
St Leonards CE Primary School, St Leonards-on-Sea

FRIENDS

Friends tell you things
Friends play with you
Friends let you play round their houses
Friends tell you secrets
Friends let you borrow things
Friends go places with you
Friends remember your birthday.

Amber Read (9)
St Leonards CE Primary School, St Leonards-on-Sea

WHAT IS PINK?

What is gold?
The sun is gold
In the morning sky.

What is green?
The grass is green
Where the slugs go by.

What is red?
A poppy is red
In its nice bed.

What is violet?
Why a violet is violet
Just a violet.

Jeffrey Eastman (10)
St Leonards CE Primary School, St Leonards-on-Sea

THE SPANISH ARMADA

Back in eighty-eight
As I do remember
Some say it was the fifth of May
But it was in November,
But it was in November.

The Spanish Armada sailed again,
With plenty of food and drink,
He got his crew drunk and then the boat sunk,
All because of their pig that's pink,
All because of their pig that's pink.

Jamie Costello (9)
St Leonards CE Primary School, St Leonards-on-Sea

CATS AND MICE

Cats and mice
They play all day
They play all night
They have a great big fight

All you can hear is
Crash, clang, squeak, miaow
Crash, clang, squeak, miaow

The mice make a wall
The cat makes a fall

Miaow

Looks like mice win.

Matthew Enoch (9)
St Leonards CE Primary School, St Leonards-on-Sea

I LIVE WITH MY . . .

I live with my mum,
I live with my dad,
I live with my brother,
That's too bad.

I live with my uncle,
I live with my aunt,
I live with my sister,
That's OK.

I live with my cat,
I live with my dog,
I live with my rabbit,
That's the best!

Amy Farnes (9)
St Leonards CE Primary School, St Leonards-on-Sea

CATS AND DOGS

Cats and dogs are so cool,
Cats are radiators,
Dogs are guards.

Cats and dogs are so cool,
Cats are soft,
Dogs are rough.

Cats and dogs are so cool,
Cats chase the mice,
Dogs chase the cats
And all you can hear
Is crash, squeak, miaow, woof,
Crash, squeak, miaow, woof
And a big
Bang!

Carol-Ann Harris (10)
St Leonards CE Primary School, St Leonards-on-Sea

IT'S SO UNFAIR!

'Mum, can I go out with some friends?'
'Jason, you're driving me round the bend.'
'At least I get to play with Zoe Statt,'
'Oh no you don't, you gotta feed the cat.'
'But Mum, I have got a social life.'
'Jason, you be cheeky and I'll get you a wife.'
'I'm begging you Mum, don't do that,
All the girls in school are fat.'
'Jason, I mean it and that's a threat.
I don't wanna feed your pet!'
It's so unfair!

Lucy Fox (10)
St Leonards CE Primary School, St Leonards-on-Sea

I HATE SHOPPING

I hate shopping at Safeways,
I hate shopping at Tesco,
I hate shopping at Iceland,
I hate shopping at New Look,
I hate shopping at W H Smith,
I hate shopping at Peacocks,
I hate shopping at B&Q,
I hate shopping at Lidl,
I hate shopping at Sainsbury's,
I hate shopping at Littlewoods,
I hate shopping with my mummy,
I hate shopping with my daddy,
I hate shopping with my nanny,
I hate shopping with my grandad.

I just hate shopping.

Kirsty Green (9)
St Leonards CE Primary School, St Leonards-on-Sea

PE

I'm in PE
I'm in PE
I'm in PE today

Balls are bouncing everywhere
Through the windows that glare

Hit the headmaster
Now he's dead
Rugby is a smashing game
Hitting everyone
Now I have won, I've got the cup.

Nathan Hyland (10)
St Leonards CE Primary School, St Leonards-on-Sea

FOOTBALL

I was on the pitch,
When I saw a ditch,
I went to see my little friend, Mitch,
Football, football, I like football.

He said to me,
What did you see
When you fouled my enemy?
Football, football, I like football.

You fouled me,
With lots of glee,
I don't know why you did it to me,
Football, football, I like football.

Darrell Moore (10)
St Leonards CE Primary School, St Leonards-on-Sea

WHAT IS PINK?

What is blue? The sea is blue
Where the sharks swim too.

What is red? Blood is red,
Trickling down a bed.

What is silver? A diamond is silver,
Lying in a house next to chicken liver.

What is gold? Why gold is just gold,
It's just gold.

Jamie Perry (9)
St Leonards CE Primary School, St Leonards-on-Sea

IT'S NEARLY CHRISTMAS

It's nearly Christmas, only two weeks to go;
It feels like the dogs are going so slow,
I just can't wait,
That's why I'm going to bed so late.

I'm hoping to get a car,
But what about my lovely rat?

Now it's the night before Christmas,
I jump in bed with a leap
And fell straight to sleep
I wake up straight away,
In the dark, I saw a white shiny bay;
Now it's morning, I open my presents,
I get lots of toys
And so do the boys.

Nikita Hilton (8)
St Mary Magdalene's RC Primary School, Bexhill-on-Sea

THE HIDDEN TREASURE

At the bottom of the sea, that's crystal clear,
A treasure you might find and it's rather near,
If you do, don't open it now,
Wait until the surface where it's safe and sound.
Once it's opened you'll be rich,
You'll even have enough to buy a football pitch.
So don't spend it quick or the fun won't last,
You'll be out of energy you'll breath and gasp.
So of it's discovered you will find,
That the hidden treasure will melt your mind.

Jack Morgan (9)
St Mary Magdalene's RC Primary School, Bexhill-on-Sea

I WOULD LIKE . . .

I would like a motorbike,
I always get a teddy
And I want a change,
I want a motorbike
In all the top range!

Everyone will look at me,
Coolest girl in the town!
They'll be laughing at Macy
With her toy clown.

I'll have loads of boyfriends running after me
Always asking me what night I'm free!
Buying me flowers,
Buying me stuff for my hair,
I'll give one clip to Macy
She will still look worse than Tony Blair!

I'll be famous and everyone will stare
If you give me a motorbike
Before you know it, I'll be sitting on the Queen's chair!

Please give me a motorbike,
Otherwise I'll cry,
If you don't I'll kill you and you will die!

Amy Gould (8)
St Mary Magdalene's RC Primary School, Bexhill-on-Sea

THAT SPECIAL SOMEONE

She helps me with my homework
Even though she shouldn't
And even when she finds it difficult
She never says couldn't

There's always a way
But she takes time to find
And when she tells me that I've got to do it
For an hour I don't really mind!

Sinead O'Brien (9)
St Mary Magdalene's RC Primary School, Bexhill-on-Sea

SISTERS

Sisters sometimes are a pest,
They really put me to the test,
Older sisters, bossing me around,
Having to listen to the latest sound.

Sisters sometimes are a pest,
They really put me to the test,
Baby sisters crying all day,
What more do I have to say?

Sisters sometimes can be kind,
Perhaps I'll have a change of mind,
When they share their sweets with me
And are nice to friends who come to tea.

Sisters sometimes aren't so bad
And then they go and make me mad,
They pull my hair, call me names,
Like to ruin all my games.

Yes sisters really are a pest,
Who daily put me to the test,
Is there any hope for me?
You'll just have to wait and see!

Christina Overbury (10)
St Mary Magdalene's RC Primary School, Bexhill-on-Sea

PETS

I would like more pets
Even though we have ten
My mum thinks it isn't suitable
Except for having a hen

In the early morning
When it's nice and bright
She'd like to find some eggs
And I'd get into a fight

I don't want a hen
I want a cute little kitten
I'd be its best mate
And this is the poem Mum would have written

I guess she'd have written it in secret
Like I have just done
But I don't think she'd have put in these words
Oh no . . . look out here comes Mum!

Alice Ball (9)
St Mary Magdalene's RC Primary School, Bexhill-on-Sea

JACKIE CHAN

One day on TV,
I was watching Jackie Chan,
Those who don't know him,
He's a really strong fighting man.

Then from out of the blue,
Flew Jackie Chan,
Hey, you remember him,
The really strong fighting man.

He told me his biggest secret,
He told me he could fly,
I told him I was just watching,
Jackie Chan who am I?

He said quickly 'Hide me,'
I screamed 'Whatever you say,'
Go to that cupboard,
That's where you will stay.

Dejuan Broughton (9)
St Mary Magdalene's RC Primary School, Bexhill-on-Sea

HIDDEN TREASURE

I am a hidden treasure,
Deep beneath the sea,
The silence of the waves do well,
Protect me, protect me.

I am a mislaid pot of gold,
Underneath the weed,
The pleasure of the dolphin shines,
Guard me, guard me.

I am a human's dream come true,
Down beneath the rocks,
The mist of sand comes clouding up,
Hide me, hide me.

All these things I am and more,
Beneath the glistening sea,
No one knows the special secret,
About me, about me.

Grace Jenkins (11)
St Mary Magdalene's RC Primary School, Bexhill-on-Sea

MY DAD

I have this dad and he
Is really cool and smart.
He never comes off his computer,
I sometimes think he's gone mad
And computer crazy.

I have this dad and he
Is mad about computers
And buildings,
Now he's a boss
But he used to be the same thing,
But not in charge of so many people.

I have this dad and he goes
So computer crazy, I think
He's an alien from outer space.

Tom Cooper (9)
St Mary Magdalene's RC Primary School, Bexhill-on-Sea

MY DREAM

As I lay tucked up in bed,
With Mummy's kiss upon my head,
I close my eyes and drift away,
To a magical land where I might play,
Where fields are green and skies are blue
And fairies dance in the morning dew,
Where rainbows end with crocks of gold
And people's hearts are never cold,
But all too soon it goes away
And it's time to wake up for another day.

Alice Johnson (10)
St Mary Magdalene's RC Primary School, Bexhill-on-Sea

MY DOLPHIN DREAM

As the dolphins dance and play,
All night long and all day,
Streaks of silver and streaks of blue,
As the water they go darting through.

Deeper down in the blue,
The dolphins want to play with you,
Jumping in and out of the sea
And leaping along to play with me.

Some are big and some are small,
All day long you hear their call,
They seem to laugh and have lots of fun
And they talk to me as they play in the sun.

I then wake up and know it's a dream,
But I keep the memory, it's so pure and clean,
I just love those dolphins wherever they are
And I hope to find them without going too far.

Hannah Wain (11)
St Mary Magdalene's RC Primary School, Bexhill-on-Sea

THE HAUNTED HOUSE

I stepped into the haunted house,
Where nothing could be heard, not even a mouse,
There was a bolt of lightning,
It was very frightening,
But there was a ghost,
Which was the scariest of the most,
So I left screaming,
With the moonlight gleaming.

Kyle Prangnell (9)
St Mary Magdalene's RC Primary School, Bexhill-on-Sea

A SCHOOL DAY

I'm going off to school today
I'll do some work and I'll play
In the playground it's such fun
We hop and skip and sometimes run
There're lots of other things to do
There's choir, there's drama and keyboard too
Back to class
Get our heads down
Or else we'll make our teacher frown
There goes the bell
It's time to fly
I wish that you could
Tell me why
Whether spent on work
Or spent on play
There are not enough
Hours in my day
There's so much more I want to do
But it's bedtime now
So goodnight to you.

Francesca Forde (9)
St Mary Magdalene's RC Primary School, Bexhill-on-Sea

MY MAGICAL WORLD

My magical world is a really nice place
It's a really good place to be
It's covered in glitter to make it look fitter
Where people are cool and funky

With magical dolphins prancing around
And with cool music there
The countries are painted with wicked colours
It's more like a magical fair

My magical world is so great
And my underwater is blue
One of my countries is luminous pink
And that's not all for you

My sky is beautiful and bright
And fishes come and dance all day
My sea is wicked too
Please, please come and play.

Ashlyn Cahill (11)
St Mary Magdalene's RC Primary School, Bexhill-on-Sea

My Mum

My mum won't let me keep a rabbit,
A toad or even a slug.
She is so mean as you can see,
Some children get to keep a flea.

I want a chicken or a duck,
I haven't got an ounce of luck.
Typical my mum is, she won't let me keep a snail
Or a gerbil with a long tail.

I want a frog but mostly a dog,
I bet you can't guess why I want a hog.
He could wallow in the pond
And of it I would be very fond.

So secretly,
I keep a bee,
In a place you wouldn't find,
In my nanna's shed, she doesn't mind.

Alice Fuller (9)
St Mary Magdalene's RC Primary School, Bexhill-on-Sea

EVERY EMMA'S WORLD

Every Emma's world
Is a joyful place to be,
Where everyone's mad and funky
And everyone acts like me.

Ages are 10 and 11,
Younger, no way you're out,
Same age definitely okay
And older, well just about.

Girls will always be welcome,
But boys I'm not so sure,
Unless they are really good-looking
And me they have to adore.

So come along for some fun,
We'll talk and we'll play
And we'll dance along for hours,
Having a good time every day.

Emma Simpson (11)
St Mary Magdalene's RC Primary School, Bexhill-on-Sea

STARDOM DREAM

I dream of being a star,
I dream of being an actress,
I dream of being famous,
I dream of being this.

An actress ever so famous,
In all the latest films,
Dancing, prancing all night long,
I can't wait to sing my song!

My dream is every child's dream,
When their imagination runs away,
So stardom please, please come to me,
It's where I'd really love to stay.

Alice Veal (10)
St Mary Magdalene's RC Primary School, Bexhill-on-Sea

AFTER SCHOOL

After school about half-past five
All the bee teachers come out of their hive
To teach all the young bees
How to make honey trees
With a buzz, buzz here
And a buzz, buzz there
They all get honey stuck in their hair

After a while they got a scare
'Cause along came a big brown bear
Who says, 'No you're doing it wrong
It's got to be like this, long and strong'
With a buzz, buzz there
And a buzz, buzz here
The bear ended up with a very sore ear

With a very sore ear
The bear felt a tear
Rolling down his cheek
The bees went to peek
With a buzz, buzz here
And a buzz, buzz there
They all felt sorry for the poor old bear.

Lana Castle (11)
St Mary Magdalene's RC Primary School, Bexhill-on-Sea

TURTLE DANCE

Sliding slowly from the bank
In the water they gracefully sank
The morning dew acts as a crystal
Turtles launch as fast as a pistol
Spying in the murky water
Ready to kill and slaughter
All the tiny fish start to spread
Out from under their sandy bed
Where turtles hide all can see
But the fish that are tiny
The turtles dance, swerve and slide
Fish swim away as they glide
Foolishly the little fish slow
Dangerously their numbers go
Going home with morning catch
To their babies that soon will hatch.

Emma Levett (11)
St Mary Magdalene's RC Primary School, Bexhill-on-Sea

MY PERSIAN CAT (THE QUEEN)

My cat Jessie
She weighs a ton
She gets very messy
But thinks she's the special one

She's very big and fluffy
I try to keep her clean
The way she sits and looks at me
She acts like she's the queen.

Rianna Clark (9)
St Mary Magdalene's RC Primary School, Bexhill-on-Sea

SCHOOL

Once I was at school on a busy day,
I just remembered it's Friday
That means I've got spellings today
I wish I was away
We've got to learn a very hard word
I don't know how to say it, so Miss, I haven't heard

At the end of the day we get time to play
I always go on Jenga because Amy G always goes mad
She sometimes can be sad

Mrs Ingram made us learn all these hard words
I wish she belonged to a family of birds.

Jessica Perry (8)
St Mary Magdalene's RC Primary School, Bexhill-on-Sea

MY DOG, DUKE

My favourite treasure is my dog, Dukey
All the time I call him Pukey,
I play with him all day,
Even when it's dull or grey.

Dukey Pukey has two bones,
I calm him down when he howls or moans,
He has great fun when he's running around,
When he sees a stranger, he's ready to pound.

Duke likes to play fun and games
And he gets called all kinds of names,
He never stops wagging his tail
And he even chews his nails!

Jessie Willis (9)
St Mary's RC Primary School, Crowborough

MY WONDERFUL CAT

I always want to keep my cat
He will be mine forever
He's always there for me
And he's really rather clever

He makes me smile and laugh
With his funny, furry slippers
I dream about him all the day
And I hope he never goes away

And when I rub his belly
It wobbles like a chunk of jelly
He munches everything with his sharp teeth
He is becoming quite a thief

My cat is a lovely snowy-white
To me he is a treasure
I'll never let him out of sight
He gives me so much pleasure.

Tyler Benton (8)
St Mary's RC Primary School, Crowborough

MY CAT

My cat sits on my lap each day,
He always wants to play.
His fur is ginger and white,
His eyes are shiny and very bright.

He is cuddly and he is fat
And he sometimes lays on our mat.
He is always happy and really sweet
And he loves to run around my feet.

Rosie Jones (8)
St Mary's RC Primary School, Crowborough

TREASURE

My treasures are my silver balls,
From when my nanny died,
Before she went she gave me her
Glittering silver balls.
In my sleep when I'm full of fear,
I try my best to keep them near,
When once I lost them,
I was panicking with fright,
But when I checked inside the cupboard,
There was a tiny glimpse of light.
It was my treasured silver balls
And ever since that frightening day,
I've had to cut down my fun and play
And keep those lovely balls away.

Connor Scarlett (8)
St Mary's RC Primary School, Crowborough

BORIS, THE CAT

My cat is a treasure to me,
Because he cares about me,
He is very soft and he is loving and loyal,
I am happy that I have got a cat
Because he comforts me at night and day
He is not very nervous and he likes Mummy's bed,
At night he rummages around the house
And pounces on our beds,
I always cuddle him.

Thomas Mitchell (8)
St Mary's RC Primary School, Crowborough

MY BABY BROTHER

I will always treasure my brother
Forever and ever
He's cute and cuddly that is true
But he is sometimes annoying to me too
I was very proud when he was born
Because I was not lonely anymore
When my mum told me
I was really excited and delighted
I really love my brother.

Shanagh Smith (9)
St Mary's RC Primary School, Crowborough

MY DOG

My dog is friendly, my dog is bold
And snuggles up when I'm cold.
My dog chases rabbits and gives them a shock,
He cocks up his ears when strangers are near.
He sleeps all day, he's awake all night,
If a burglar broke in, they'd never come back.
So we'll stick together for evermore.

Brian O'Connor (9)
St Mary's RC Primary School, Crowborough

MY TENT

I treasure my tent a lot,
Because it's fun to put up and be in,
When I enter my tent I feel safe,
Joyful and happy.

I go in my tent when I'm happy,
I go in my tent when I'm sad,
I go in my tent when I'm grumpy
And especially when I'm mad.

Charlie Nicoll (9)
St Mary's RC Primary School, Crowborough

MY TREASURE

My rabbit is my treasure,
She has always been,
She's cute and cuddly and that is how she's seen.
It was her birthday last Sunday,
We bought her a treat,
She ate and ate as if it was a sweet.

My rabbit is my treasure,
She has a sister just the same,
They like to have a lot of fun
By playing silly games.
They run around the garden, jumping over walls,
Eating grass and having fun and getting messy paws.

My rabbit is my treasure
And Toyah is her name,
When she's sweet I give her a treat,
But remember not to give her meat.
We open the door of the rabbit's cage,
Jumpity jump the rabbits come,
Hello again, another day of fun.

Natasha Beard (8)
St Mary's RC Primary School, Crowborough

THE MAGIC DUSTBIN

My treasure is my bin,
It opens when I'm near,
I play inside, it's quite alive.
It's even got a bed,
I sleep for a while,
When I wake, I play with my toys.

I never felt lonely,
Not even scared,
I'm full of surprises,
I play with some games,
Then I watch a video.

When it rains, I come back in
And I keep my secret forever and ever.

Tyler Andrews (8)
St Mary's RC Primary School, Crowborough

COMBAT TROUSERS

My combat trousers will never go
Because I've worn them so and so
My mum says they've reached the end
But I say . . . No!

I've used and used them through the years
I wore them at Brighton pier
Got to go says my mum
On them my dad spilt rum, eek!

Jojo Kyne (9)
St Mary's RC Primary School, Crowborough

MY INVISIBLE FRIEND

Sitting on my bed is a sort of friend you know,
You can't see him
You can't hear his voice
But you can talk to him, in a sort of way

He's always good, never bad
He does what I say every day
All day he tidies my room and he never complains

I'm always going to keep him
Whatever I do
He's going to be my friend forever and ever

I'm never going to let him go
He's my invisible friend.

Harry Wrigley (8)
St Mary's RC Primary School, Crowborough

MY TEDDY BEARS

I'll never get rid of my teddy bears
Even ones with boring glares
I go crazy whenever one gets lost
Doesn't matter how much it cost

I treasure my Lego
It's good to put together
I will never give it away
Never, never, never.

Jonathan Townhill (9)
St Mary's RC Primary School, Crowborough

MY TEDDY BEAR

I'm always going to keep my ted,
I have it safe in bed.
I treasure it because it's mine
And I've kept it since I was tiny.

When I'm scared and have nightmares,
I cuddle it with fright.
I've always wondered why I care
So much for my teddy bear.

Sam Morgan (8)
St Mary's RC Primary School, Crowborough

MY TREASURE

My treasure is my mum and dad
Who wipe my tears away
They tuck me up in bed at night
And teach me how to play
The best thing about my mum and dad
Is that they treasure me.

Lydia Shepherd (8)
St Mary's RC Primary School, Crowborough

MY DREAMCATCHER

I will always keep my dreamcatcher,
It's mine and it's my favourite treasure,
It has always taken my bad dreams away
And I will keep it forever and ever.

I go to bed when it's night
And dream I'm far away,
When I wake, a day's gone by,
That's all I'm going to say.

Charlotte Edwards (9)
St Mary's RC Primary School, Crowborough

MY DREAM CATCHER

I really love my dreamcatcher,
It takes my bad dreams away,
When I am upset and full of fear,
I look up to it night and day.

It twinkles in the moonlight,
When I am asleep in bed,
Although I cannot feel it,
It takes the bad dreams out of my head.

Lydia Bannister (9)
St Mary's RC Primary School, Crowborough

WHEN I WAS . . .

When I was one I'd just begun,
When I was two I'd learnt to chew,
When I was three I fell out of a tree,
When I was four I bumped my head on the door,
When I was five I felt alive,
When I was six I worshipped 'Steps',
When I was seven I felt eleven,
Now I'm eight
I feel great!

Lauren Smith (8)
St Peter & St Paul Primary School, Bexhill-on-Sea

SEASONS

The green grass is blowing,
Leaves twirling to the ground,
Falling softly down,
With a rustling sound.

Silently snow falls,
Carpeting the world in white,
Sprinkling shimmering stars,
That dance in the moonlight.

As the earth awakens
To the buzzing bee,
Beautiful pink blossom
Decorates the trees.

Sparkling golden sunshine,
Clear skies of blue,
The smell of fresh-cut meadows
And time off school too!

Jessica Elliott (8)
St Peter & St Paul Primary School, Bexhill-on-Sea

ROBOTS

R   obots are capable machines
O   perated by brain and by wires
B   ut there is one problem, they aren't graceful
O   ver and over again will do what you want
T   hey help you
S   tanding there silently.

Kieron Akam (9)
St Peter & St Paul Primary School, Bexhill-on-Sea

OH NO!

The whirling noise of the siren breaks the silence,
It's gone, it's gone off, oh no!
I rush to the air raid shelter,
Quick, quick says a voice in my body,
I'm in, phew! I'm safe now.
Bang! I cuddle my mum. I ask will our house still be there?
What if it isn't? What will we do?
'I don't know,' my mum replies.
I hope the firemen and the soldiers are okay.
I hear some children crying,
Some screaming bombs, I'm really terrified.
I burst into tears, my mum comforts me,
She makes me feel warm and protected,
'It's okay, we're safe in here,' she says.

Megan Milarski (8)
St Peter & St Paul Primary School, Bexhill-on-Sea

ROBOTS

Robots are automated machines
Operated by wires
And they have arms
That look just like pliers
Their joints clank as they glide around
They hiss and zoom right along the ground

There once was a robot
Who went to the sky
He had red eyes and silver joints
Oh how he did fly!

Chloé Lusted (9)
St Peter & St Paul Primary School, Bexhill-on-Sea

MY HERO!

James Bond is my hero
And Q I do like too
He makes the cars and weapons that
James Bond will need to use
My favourite film I've seen
'Tomorrow Never Dies'
Is full of guns and bombs and things
And villains and bad guys!
I know the job to do
When I have finished school
A secret agent – that's for me
It really would be *cool!*

Aaron Pape (8)
St Peter & St Paul Primary School, Bexhill-on-Sea

WEATHER

The weather is swirling
Round and round
The wind is twirling a tune for me
It's starting to rain
Isn't it a pain?
I better go in or I'll get wet through!
I hear leaves drinking
I hear rain dropping
I hear the rain sliding silently from the leaves
Drop, drop.

Jennie Warnett (8)
St Peter & St Paul Primary School, Bexhill-on-Sea

WHO'S THE MONSTER?

The monster behind the loo
Is camouflaged – I'm telling you
But when you sit down
You can see a great hand –
And his bright yellow feet
Poke out too!

James Taylor (8)
St Peter & St Paul Primary School, Bexhill-on-Sea

ROBOTS

R   obots so neat and shiny
O   ther robots fat and thin
B   odies twist round and round
O   ver-working machines
T   wist and turn
S   hiny, cheerful machines.

Faith Young (9)
St Peter & St Paul Primary School, Bexhill-on-Sea

THE ROBOT

There it was
Its tiny red eyes
Seemed to watch me
It whizzed towards me
Humming loudly
My mind raced
A robot!

Helen Johnson (8)
St Peter & St Paul Primary School, Bexhill-on-Sea

THE 20 TON CHOCOLATE MOUNTAIN

He'd done it, he'd won the race,
He uttered to himself
'You're here Tom,
You're at the 20 ton chocolate mountain.'

Signs came in his line of vision
With the words
Beware! Sinking syrup
On them.
And he was almost hit by an oncoming fairy cake
That actually flew!

He was tempted to go for a swim at the
Newly opened strawberry milkshake pool.
But didn't want to climb the jagged
White chocolate pyramids.

He stood back,
The mountains loomed over him,
A layer of marzipan started it off,
Next up, candyfloss,
Surrounded by drizzling cream.
It was lit by butterscotch candles
And oozing fudge.

Tom knew he would be spending his days
Within the treasure of the
20 ton chocolate mountain.

Dominic Pearson (11)
Somerhill Junior School

FACES

I look around,
Faces everywhere,
Two eyes,
Two ears,
A mouth and a nose,
But
All
So
Different.
Angry faces,
    Happy faces,
        Sad faces,
    Young faces,
Old faces,
        Spotty faces,
    Pretty faces,
        Dirty faces,
Clean faces.

I can tell some people think they're ugly,
But they're not,
I say,
'No one's ugly,
Everybody has their own treasure
And that's
    Their
        Own
            Special
                Features.'

Dara Brown (11)
Somerhill Junior School

HIDDEN TREASURE

I'm sailing on a deep blue sea,
Water splashing over me!
Day becomes dusk,
Sun hidden by candyfloss.
The sky is a developing bruise,
So far this is a supreme island cruise.
My boat is tilting to and fro,
Rocking and rocking,
The waves are rough.
I'm getting near to paradise.
The water looks like frozen ice!
Sand has surrounded a thin palm tree,
The leaves are green,
My boat has crashed and I look forward
And there is sand,
A magical exotic island land,
An island gem just waiting to be found.
I can't wait to look around.
This is my hidden treasure; oh it's such a pleasure.
I've always wanted to discover something new,
But this is my dream come true.

Lucy Udeen (10)
Somerhill Junior School

BURIED TREASURE

Buried treasure is all I want,
Lovely jubbly treasure!
All the things that I could have
Lovely jubbly treasure!

It really is just all I need,
Lovely jubbly treasure!
Oh! Look I've found my
Buried treasure!
It's super-duper treasure!

Rosemary Coogan (10)
Somerhill Junior School

MY CLASS

I once knew a boy called Tom,
Who threw a stink bomb.

The bomb hit a boy called Reece,
Who turned to Tom and said, 'Peace.'

Tom then threw one at Freddie,
Who cried and hugged his teddy.

Then he chased a girl called Grace,
But he could not keep up at her pace.

Tom then threw a bomb at Marna
And hit her because she slipped on a banana.

He then aimed for Sam,
But instead he hit an old man.

In the end Tom was in tears,
Because his mum pulled him home by his ears.

Ned Butcher (10)
Stonegate CE Primary School

MY PONY

I've got a pony,
A very pretty pony.

I do her water,
A litre and a quarter.

Then I do her hay,
For two times a day.

I love horses,
Especially doing cross-country courses.

I put her to bed,
Being careful not to bump her head.

Shutting the door of her stable,
As quiet as I am able.

Lucy Jordan (9)
Stonegate CE Primary School

MY PONY, JET

Up, up and away on my jet-black steed,
Over jumps at tremendous speed.

Winning all the races,
At the fastest of paces.

Then when we go home,
I set Jet out to roam.

At the end of the day,
We had so much fun,
My pony, Jet is the greatest one.

Amy Smith (9)
Stonegate CE Primary School

DREAMING

A bump in the night,
A flash of light,
I shiver,
I dither,
I jump with a fright.
A clatter,
A scatter,
I scream and scream.
I open my eyes,
Phew . . .
It was just a dream.

Jessica Steven (9)
Stonegate CE Primary School

MY DOG

I love my dog called Todd
He's a very woolly sort of dog
He rounds up our sheep
With a bound and a dart and a leap

He has short, stumpy legs and lots of whiskers on his head
He plays a lot with our new pup called Sky
Round and round together they fly
I hope she will be as good as Todd
He really is a clever sort of dog.

Tom Wortley (10)
Stonegate CE Primary School

RAT

Quick cat!
Catch that rat,
Through my room, along the broom,
Over the glass,
Through the grass.
Miaow,
Squeak.
Through the butter, up the gutter,
Round the house,
Oh no, there's a mouse.
Quick cat,
Catch that rat,
Before it gets too fat!

Henry Bramall (10)
Stonegate CE Primary School

BUILDING

The sound of the crane spinning around
The sound of the bricks hitting the ground

The sound of the cement swirling fast
The sound of the birds flying past

The sound of the digger digging up mud
The sound of the spade landing with a thud

The sound of the rocks flying through the air
But the diggers, they just don't care.

Toby Longhurst (9)
Stonegate CE Primary School

POOR LITTLE CAT

The cat thunders across the ground,
Making a terrible rumbling sound.
The bird races through the air,
Chasing the cat, he's nearly there!
A tail trails behind the cat,
Out he goes, through the flap.
Up the chimney the bird goes,
Through the air, like a river he flows.
He sees the cat up a tree,
What a brilliant place to be.
He'll have to stay there,
It's too high to jump,
But he did and landed in a lump.
Splat!
That poor little cat.

Joseph Pocock (10)
Stonegate CE Primary School

BUILDING

Diggers running wild, scooping up mud,
Bricks are piled in stacks,
Trucks are coming in and out,
Builders have weary backs.

Cranes are whizzing through the air,
Thick mud is on the ground,
The dumper truck is very strong,
Rubbish is piled in a mound.

Megan Brickell (10)
Stonegate CE Primary School

THE SEASIDE SUICIDE

Gulls swoop and sweep and swipe around me
As if they will feed on my dead body
My family try to stop me jumping
But they know as I do, it's too late
The splashing, crashing, mashing of the waves
Will be the last sound I hear
I jump
And fall
And fall
And fall
And see on the great blue ocean
A glittering face smirking at me
Splat!

Fred Maynard (11)
Stonegate CE Primary School

I HAVE A HORSE

I have a horse who likes to trot
Clippity-clop
Clippity-clop

I have a horse who likes to eat
Yum yum
In his tum

I have a horse who likes to jump
Over the jump
And far away.

Sophie Mallion (10)
Stonegate CE Primary School

NO FUN WHEN BULLOCKS RUN

As I enter the field, I stop and stare
Then I see a bullock there,
I creep,
I crawl,
I trip over,
I fall.
But then,
Oh dear,
The bull has a sharp ear,
He runs,
He sprints,
I turn, I flee.
I *run!*
Over the fence, over the wall,
Over the hills, down the road,
Home at last, safe and sound.

Peter Snow (11)
Stonegate CE Primary School

THE DUCK

Behold the duck,
It does not cluck,
A duck it lacks
Its quacks,
It is especially fond
Of a puddle or a pond,
When it dives or sups,
It bottoms up.

Millie Shreeve (10)
Stonegate CE Primary School

A RECIPE FOR SPRING!

Take the sun
Primroses and bluebells
A bud on a tree
Melting snow
Mix it in a cauldron
Simmer for 24 hours
And then you'll have . . .
Spring!

Charlotte Wates (9)
Stonegate CE Primary School

IN THE SKY

Flying high in the air,
Looking down, I do not dare,
I see the shapes up in the sky
And all the birds just flutter by.

Alix Longhurst (9)
Stonegate CE Primary School

MY BIG BROTHER

My big brother is very cool
He has a great big ball
Because he loves playing football
My brother, James loves playing games
He shames my mum so.

Grace Lane (9)
Stonegate CE Primary School

STANDING STILL

I stand still like a tree
the breeze comes through my leaves

The air can be cold like the North Pole
and it can be silent in the morning

I've got an enormous trunk to keep me grounded.

Mana Pettyl (10)
Stonegate CE Primary School

TANK

The great iron belly rumbles across fields,
Anything which gets in its way is smashed,
Crash!
It has a trunk bigger than any elephant,
Scales tougher than any crocodile,
This machine is the greatest of all.

Christopher Steven (11)
Stonegate CE Primary School

MAX

There was a young boy called Max,
Whose eyes melted you like candle wax,
He had a brown, button nose
And dainty shell-pink toes,
His hair was the colour of flax.

Sophie Rolleston-Smith (10)
Stonegate CE Primary School

MY MAGIC BOX

The baa of a sheep when it's happy,
My dog barking outside in the dark,
The taste of my strawberries when sugar's on them.

I will put in my magic box
Seeing the river flowing among the lilies,
The feel of sheep's fur when it feels like it,
The ducks quacking in the pond.

I will put in my magic box
The smell of flowers when they are new,
The rustle of the trees rustling in the wind,
The spots on a cheetah.

Theo Briffa (9)
Temple Grove School

MY MAGIC BOX

I will put in my magic box
My mum's smiling face first thing in the morning
The smell of my dad's aftershave
The wind blowing on a Saturday night

I will put in my magic box
The smell of my mum's cooking in the kitchen
The feel of warm air against my mum's face
The feel of dogs' hair

I will put in my magic box
The hot sun on a summer's day
The sound of Beatles music
The colours of the sunset.

Jack Vickers (9)
Temple Grove School

MY MAGIC BOX

The taste of an apple on a summer afternoon
The sound of a clock chiming at noon
The strength of a knife carving a stick

I will put in my magic box
The air you breathe clear as day
The warmth of the fire on a cold winter's night
The sound of music out of a CD player

I will put in my magic box
The sound of people's voices in the television screen
The rain spitting down on a cold day
The works of art and pictures in books.

Henry Mawhood (8)
Temple Grove School

MY MAGIC BOX

I will put in my magic box
The smell of a baby's hair when it's just been washed
The power and the magic of a unicorn's horn
The sound of the birds on a winter's day

I will put in my magic box
The sight of a dolphin jumping in the sea
The feeling of the wind blowing on my face
The beauty of a princess sitting in a castle

I will put in my magic box
The sight of flowers in a big green field
The sunset by the ocean as it twinkles in the sea
And watching the world enjoying themselves.

Larah Ann Charlesworth (9)
Temple Grove School

MAGIC BOX

I will put in my magic box
My baby cousin's hug when I'm upset
The horn of a unicorn with magic inside
The song of Christmas on a snowy evening

I will put in my magic box
The sound of children laughing loudly on a summer's day
The soft wind of a summer's night
The sound of waves in the Atlantic

I will put in my magic box
The sound of winter fairies in a wood
The lake whistling through a field
The brightest orange of a sunset
The smell of paint when wet.

Jessica Barrett (9)
Temple Grove School

MY MAGIC BOX

I will put in my magic box
The taste of a hot chilli
The smell of chocolate being cooked
The feel of dog's hair when I stroke it

I will put in my magic box
The sound of TV when it's on
The feel of the wind on my face
The sound of the birds in the morning

I will put in my magic box
The sound of the wind and the sea
The taste of the juicy and sweet mussels
The day my brother was born.

Ben Mundy (8)
Temple Grove School

MY MAGIC BOX

I will put in my magic box
The loving hug of my mum on a joyful day
The smell of hot treacle running down a bowl
The sound of the wind blowing into my ear

I will put in my magic box
The bitterest lemon in the country
The softness of my brother's skin against my fingers
The colours of a rainbow high in the sky

I will put in my magic box
The buzz of a bee echoing through the air
A sip from the cold, refreshing water of Loch Ness
The feel of hot chocolate trickling down my throat

That is what I will put in my magic box.

Sam Balcombe (9)
Temple Grove School

MY MAGIC WEB

I will put in my magic box
The summer's sun in the morning
The smell of sweets in a shop
The warm air of hot summer days

I will put in my magic box
The hair of my dog at home
The sound of a woodpecker pecking
The feel of the bark of a tree

I will put in my magic box
The roar of a dinosaur fighting
The smell of petrol when my mum puts it in
The smell of fire when it is lit
The smile of my mum!

William McCrow (8)
Temple Grove School

MY MAGIC BOX

I will put in my magic box

The taste of cabbage at dinner time
Seeing a picture of The Amber Room
The noise of a woodpecker just before night

I will put in my box

The look of crystals when they sparkle
The look of cobwebs with dew on
The feel of butterflies in my tummy

I will put in my magic box

The noise of the wind through the trees
The smell of cakes in the kitchen
The feel of gloves when they are warm.

Amber Jenkins (8)
Temple Grove School

MY MAGIC BOX

I will put in my magic box
The bark of an angry dog
The nice taste of chicken tikka
The stroke of soft fur

I will put in my magic box
To see the bright sunset
The really nice fur of a cat
The taste of yummy ice cream

I will put in my magic box
The sweet baa of a sheep
The lovely taste of a cheeseburger
The sound of trees rustling
And the cute look of animals.

Charlie Dagwell (9)
Temple Grove School

MY MAGIC BOX

In my magic box I will put . . .

The feel of my cat, Mew-Mew's fur by the fire,
The feel of a warm shower after a cold day in winter,
The smell of melted chocolate from a factory.

I will put in the box . . .

The feel of cramming large amounts of cucumber into my mouth,
The pop of an experiment from my science kit,
The feel of gelled hair in the morning.

I will put in the box . . .

The smell of fruit from the bowl,
The taste of raspberries picked by me,
The texture of slime from my slime lab.

Jesse Asherson-Webb (9)
Temple Grove School

MY DAY

My day is lovely, I watch the sun come up every day,
I get dressed and have my breakfast

I get ready to walk to school,
I walk to school and when I get there,
I do the register and start the day

I do school for six hours
And walk home, then I play my computer
And go to bed whilst watching a video.

Danny Taylor (11)
West Hove Junior School

HIDDEN TREASURE

My hidden treasure is love,
It is deep down in my heart.
It flies within me like a dove,
It pierces me like a dart.

My hidden treasure is love,
It grows in me like a flower.
It flies in me like a dove,
It grows by the hour.

My hidden treasure is love,
It attracts insects good and bad.
It flies within me like a dove,
Things I'll have and things that I've had.

My hidden power is love,
It comes in the morning.
It flies within me like a dove,
Just as the day is dawning.

Jack Smith (10)
West Hove Junior School

THINK OF LOST CHILDREN!

When you sit there thinking, parents' hearts are sinking,
Wondering why their children haven't come home.
You can tell something's gone on,
When you're thinking of your father, Ron,
When he once hadn't come home.
So say in your head, think of all the lost children
And thank God that yours have come home.

Chelsea Richards (11)
West Hove Junior School

BURIED TREASURE

I went to a cave to find some treasure,
More than I can ever measure.
Jewels, diamonds, pearls and gold,
Enough to last me till I'm old.

I hope that an 'X' marked the spot,
For that was the whole point of the plot.
I dug and dug until my fingers bled,
But all I found were the bones of the dead.

I saw a box, it looked like treasure,
Perhaps this was my time for pleasure.
I picked it up and opened the case,
But all I found was an old shoelace!

Louis Dodd (10)
West Hove Junior School

THE BEACH

On a summer's day,
Kids and grown-ups are swimming in the sea,
You can see the horizon as clear as can be,
Ice creams are melting, seagulls are flying,
The sun is burning over the sea.

On a windy day,
The waves are rough, the sea is tough,
Splashing over the rocks as hard as can be,
The wind is blowing, a tidal wave's growing,
The wind is blowing over the sea.

Jamie Milton (10)
West Hove Junior School

THE HIDDEN TREASURE

I see the scuttling squirrels
Gathering up the winter's store,
Nibbling a few nuts now and then,
Then hopping back for more.

I see them all exhausted
At the end of the day,
From the hard work, dodging cats and dogs
And chasing birds away.

I see the starving squirrels
In the garden that is bare,
No nuts or berries on the tree,
No food for them to share.

I see them scurry down the tree
And scrabble on the ground,
The treasure hidden months ago
Has now at last been found.

Georgina Cluett (10)
West Hove Junior School

I WONDER

I wonder about my mum
I wonder about my dad
I always knew about my sister
The sister I should never have had!

I wonder about my teacher
I wonder about the Head
I wonder about my friends
Even when stuck in my bed!

I wonder about TV stars
I wonder about Michael Owen
I wonder about everything
I even wonder about this poem!

Emma Peat (11)
West Hove Junior School

HIDDEN TREASURE

The hidden treasure lies close somewhere,
Under the big, clear, blue water lair.
All the creatures near the sea,
Might reach it just before me.

The great sperm whale,
Is bound not to fail.
He can wag his tail,
As he travels along his treasure trail.

The great white shark,
Travels alone in the dark,
Because he's planning away,
So he gets there before the start of a new day.

The sly stingray,
Is bound to find his way,
He will float along the ocean floor,
Then he'll sweep into the treasure tower door.

The hidden treasure lies close somewhere,
Under the big, clear, blue water lair.
All the creatures near the sea,
Might reach it just before me.

Blue Dean Keeter (11)
West Hove Junior School

SEA MOODS

The clouds and sky get darker and darker,
As dark as dark will ever be.
As yet again the rain will pour into the
Deadly, deadly sea.

Reflections start to disappear
As the water starts to churn,
Fishermen turn their tails and run
As the sea begins to burn.

The sea is water, lethal water,
With the sound of a million booming mortars.

Crash, boom, go the raging waves,
As lightning fills the coves and caves.

Suck, flush sings the sea, suck flush it sings,
Bringing up waves that it always brings.

Armies of white horses gallop through,
Dragging shingle and driftwood too.

The waves tire and start to shrink,
As through the clouds, the sun starts to wink.

Heaven opens its gates on the ocean,
As people all around get their smiles in motion.

Levi Ryder Bianco (11)
West Hove Junior School

HIDDEN TREASURES

My hidden treasure is shiny and gold,
I always get it out to look at and hold.

My hidden treasure is all necklaces and rings,
I hide it in with all my other things.

My hidden treasure is hidden in my drawer,
I found it in an olden-day store.

My hidden treasure is very old,
I have to look after it, I keep getting told.

Hannah Rhodes (10)
West Hove Junior School

MY CAT

My cat is black, as black as night,
With tufty ears and a fluffy tail,
That you shouldn't pull or else he'll bite
And teeth like fangs, hurts like hell.

He pads around on his dainty paws,
Looking for a comfortable place to nap,
Oh no! Mum, he's in my drawers,
Where do I put clean clothes now?

When he's playful, he is quite mad,
Chasing toy mice and a silver ball,
Up and down the stairs, then skidding into Dad,
Making Dad jump and shout, he is silly though.

His fur feels like nice warm silk,
Soft and smooth, it glistens when he moves,
Especially when he's lapping his favourite milk,
Or pleading to be fed, again!

Sometimes he's a nuisance, but I don't mind,
I give him lots of love and care,
My cat is definitely one of a kind,
I love Sylvester, I'm so glad he's mine.

Gavin Barsby (10)
West Hove Junior School

HIDDEN TREASURES

Under the sea
An octopus lays
On a treasure chest locked up

The octopus with eight legs is big
And covers the whole treasure chest
The octopus is so big you only see
A glimpse of gold

I once got past the octopus
And I found the chest
I swam to the shore
And looked at the chest
Where was the key?

I looked at the soft sand
And thought *could the key be there?*
I dug very hard in the sand
And lifted out the key

I expected a gold crown
And silver money, but alas
I found shrimps and lovely things
For the octopus
I swam and gave the octopus
Back his treasure chest.

Yasmine Sebbah (7)
West Hove Junior School

WINTER

Falling snow on the ground
Winter walking all around
Icy fingers and icy toes
Grabbing sleeves of children's clothes

Its frozen breath freezes you
Makes you cold and turns you blue
Slowing traffic and having fun
The day is spoiled when out comes the sun.

Charlotte Janay Burton (10)
West Hove Junior School

MY SECRET GARDEN

My secret garden
Is hidden far away
No one can find it
Because only I know the way

I go there when I want to dream
I flow through just like steam
My secret garden is hard to find
Because it's locked in my mind.

Mason Horgan (10)
West Hove Junior School

SECRET TREASURES

There's a secret treasure in everyone,
a treasure deep inside,
it makes you happy and sad,
this treasure no one can hide.
It helps your mind, body and soul,
through every passing day,
it lays beneath your skin,
helping you in every way.
This secret treasure helps you and me,
your individuality!

Nadia Wareham (10)
West Hove Junior School

TREASURE ISLAND

My magnificent boat like a huge floating sea monster,
Is going towards the mysterious island,
With trees full of exotic fruits and rare animals!
The musical birds like a great band,
Whistle! Chirp! Flutter!
It is boiling, it is sunny,
Oh, too good to be true!
Waves like long arms, waving goodbye,
Splashing towards the island like lions pouncing and roaring!
The glorious froth is as white as snow, but as cold as ice.
The sea controlled by Neptune's fingers is all around me.
Until I finally find it beneath the silky, soft, golden sand,
The treasure chest full of gold, silver, crowns, rubies and diamonds,
Sparkling and glittering like stars!
I am finally rich!

Harriet Massing (8)
West Hove Junior School

MY SISTER

'We've got some news for you'
Mum and Dad said with a grin,
'Something you've always wanted'
A sister for me, yippee!

She kept me awake at night
Always cried and cried and cried
It wouldn't of been so bad
If she didn't share my room

And as she got a little bit older
Naughty wasn't the word
She always got me into trouble
But it was her who broke all my toys

If only I'd never mentioned
A sister would be nice
I'd still have peace and quiet
But I suppose she's worth the sacrifice.

Daisy Penfold (10)
West Hove Junior School

HOLIDAYS

Holidays are such fun, it makes treats for everyone
Girls and boys saying hello to you
All looking for things to do
Eating ice cream and candy stuff
But drinking a lot is never enough
Swimming in the cool blue sea
Making sandcastles for you and me
Getting ready for an all-night party
Dancing shoes moving in time
To the rhythm of music divine
Globes circles sending out colour in every space
People dancing from every race
At last the time has come to go to bed
To refresh ourselves for the day ahead
When the holiday is finally over and done
We look forward to next holiday's fun.

Shanita Limbachia (11)
West Hove Junior School

HIDDEN TREASURES

When I was on holiday
We went diving in a bay,
We were told a story of a map,
That the captain had on his lap.

It revealed the way
To the end of the bay,
Where there lay a shipwreck,
You could see from the deck.

We went to have a look,
But we were shocked,
When we saw a chest,
So we told the rest.

We dived down into the sea
And swam to the chest to see,
Emeralds, diamonds and gold,
Just as the captain had told.

James Murdoch (11)
West Hove Junior School

THE PIGGARUMBULL!

I saw the Piggarumbull
Outside my house one day,
I saw the Piggarumbull
Outside one day in May.

I looked at the Piggarumbull
And it looked at me,
Outside my house one day in May,
It was a funny sight to see!

Aeron Corrigan (10)
West Hove Junior School

PHOENIX SUN

The phoenix flies as dawn creeps in,
His colours shine bright,
For the world is dim.

Gold, orange, pink and red,
The colours shine brightly in the light,
The world is waking from slumber in bed.

As the day progresses, so does he,
Climbing towards the cloud,
No one can see him, not even the trees.

As dusk approaches, he's falling fast,
They come to watch in a crowd,
Coming to a halt, he saves himself from death
Does he part.

And so he sinks down into the hills,
A beautiful sight to see,
The curtains rest on the window sills,
The world is at peace and so is he.

Lucy Donaldson (11)
West Hove Junior School

THE SEA

The sea is like a silver star shining in the sky.
The sea is like a rainbow all different colours.
The sea is like a zoo looking after loads of animals.
The sea is in our lives forever and in our hearts forever.
The sea is a giant bowl of water.
The sea is God's tears of joy.
The sea is the *sea!*

Darryl Simmonds
West Hove Junior School

HIDDEN TREASURES

Over the fresh, green hilltops
Over the long, golden crops
Behind the trees, standing tall
I saw a room, round and small.

Gold, jewels were laid upon the door
And then I knew there was more
I opened the door to see
The whole place was full of glee

There were castles of gold
Strips of fine silver were rolled
Little elves were working there
And one had a moment to spare

'The treasures are all here'
He said with a slight sneer
'There are ancient and new ones
Quick, the monster's coming, run!'

'Quick, go back where you came from!'
I ran home to village Crom
I told the village my stay
But that's as far as I can say

So that's the hidden treasures
Yet it is all very true
Secret, it will be no more
For it is opened up to you.

Monwara Malik (11)
West Hove Junior School

HIDDEN TREASURES!

Far more beautiful than you have ever seen
Purple, red, gold, silver, blue and green
These are the colours of wonderful animals
Tiny or huge but gorgeous animals
Look very closely and you will see
The wonderful hidden treasures there'll be
Butterflies' wings are multicoloured
Shiny, sparkly, magnificently coloured
Beetles come in all sizes and tones
Glistening, sleek, metallic tones
The fantastic birds that fly in the sky
Are beautiful with sharp, pretty eyes
The frogs and toads that all go croak
Have all sorts of browns and greens on their coats
The flowers brightly bloom and gently sway
Their outstanding colours showing every day
The night is beautiful and sparkly and new
With badgers and owls and mice among dew
These are hidden treasures because at first glance
You cannot tell their beauty except by chance
These treasures remain hidden if you always rush
But if you go for a peaceful walk
Just stretching your legs and no talk
The animals will come out and up to you
They will show their amazing treasures to you
You can crouch, bend, look up or peek
You can examine the treasures small or sleek
One day try this in a forest or field
The hidden treasures will all be revealed!

Parisah Seyed-Safi (11)
West Hove Junior School

ANOTHER DAY

And here comes another day
Not to stay for too long
On it goes, round and round
Till it reaches another place
Hourly through time and pace
Every day it comes up
Ready to get brightened up

Dawn has come, it's settled now
And it's quite a sight right now
Yearly it comes because it's another day.

Stacey Mair (11)
West Hove Junior School

CASTLES AT WAR

Boom! Boom! Boom, the drums alert,
'Fire!' orders the sergeant,
Boom! bellows the canon,
Crumble! fall the walls of the castle,
Chop! swing the swordsmen.
Bang! fires the gunman,
Roar! yells the dragon of the deep,
Ping! fly the arrows,
Splash! whooshes the castle's moat,
Yeah! cheer the winners of the war.

Lewis Husbands (10)
West Hove Junior School

HIDDEN TREASURE

On my hunt
To find my treasure
I met a man
He was a beggar

I took him with me
Throughout
My journey

We travelled through
Caves and mountain
Passes

I found the treasure
But he stole it from me
And I never saw him again.

Steven Trafford (11)
West Hove Junior School